SELLING OUT THE SPECTRUM

of related interest

The Autism and Neurodiversity Self Advocacy Handbook
Developing the Skills to Determine Your Own Future
Yenn Purkis and Barb Cook
ISBN 978 1 78775 575 8
eISBN 978 1 78775 576 5

Taking off the Mask
Practical Exercises to Help Understand and Minimise
the Effects of Autistic Camouflaging
Dr Hannah Louise Belcher
Foreword by Will Mandy, PhD, DClinPsy
ISBN 978 1 78775 589 5
eISBN 978 1 78775 590 1

Autistic and Black
Our Experiences of Growth, Progress and Empowerment
Kala Allen Omeiza
ISBN 978 1 83997 620 9
eISBN 978 1 83997 621 6

Autistic World Domination
How to Script Your Life
Jolene Stockman
ISBN 978 1 83997 444 1
eISBN 978 1 83997 445 8

SELLING OUT THE SPECTRUM

How Science Lost the Trust of Autistic People, and How It Can Win It Back

Liam O'Dell

Jessica Kingsley Publishers
London and Philadelphia

First published in Great Britain in 2025 by Jessica Kingsley Publishers
An imprint of John Murray Press

1

Content Warning: This book mentions bullying, eugenics, conversion
therapy, trauma, racism, ableism, transphobia and abuse.

A CIP catalogue record for this title is available from the
British Library and the Library of Congress

ISBN 978 1 83997 626 1
eISBN 978 1 83997 627 8

Printed and bound in Great Britain by TJ Books Limited

Jessica Kingsley Publishers' policy is to use papers that are natural,
renewable and recyclable products and made from wood grown in
sustainable forests. The logging and manufacturing processes are expected
to conform to the environmental regulations of the country of origin.

Jessica Kingsley Publishers
Carmelite House
50 Victoria Embankment
London EC4Y 0DZ

www.jkp.com

John Murray Press
Part of Hodder & Stoughton Ltd
An Hachette Company

For the unashamedly curious...

Contents

Acknowledgements

Given the seriousness and importance of its subject matter, I made sure to strip this book of inappropriate hyperbole, and that applies here. I am not exaggerating when I say that it has been an ambition since childhood to have a book published – anyone who knows me well enough and for long enough will know that. Now that has been achieved, there are a handful of people to thank.

My family, who nurtured an undiagnosed autistic boy's special interest in reading and writing from the very beginning. The brilliant English teachers over the years who have encouraged my love for and fascination with the English language, and those who during my time in education would gladly receive a chapter or two of a work in progress, only for doubt in my creative ability to result in my abandoning the idea just a few weeks later. Special thanks must go to my secondary school careers advisor, Ms Armstrong, whose recommendation to start up a blog in 2012 triggered a chain of events which have led me to the privileged position in which I now find myself, and to Mr Eager, to whom my parents and I are forever indebted.

I am grateful to Alanna Collen, for her advice and support, and to my local writers' group, who have cheered me on whenever I have been able to make a meeting. My thanks, too, to

Emily Faint. I promised you a dedication in my next book, but in case I become the literary version of a one-hit wonder, I want to note my gratitude here. Your friendship during the turbulent process of writing this book, and genuine excitement for it to be out in the world, motivated me immensely.

Thank you to everyone who kindly contributed to this project – especially all the autistic interviewees who placed their trust in me to handle such an urgent and delicate issue with care and sensitivity.

My thanks to my brilliant editorial team at Jessica Kingsley Publishers, comprising Lisa Clark, Isabel Martin, Abbie Howard and Lynda Cooper. To Judy Napper, for copyediting both versions of my manuscript. To Victoria Peters and Claire Robinson, who saw this book through the production process. Ian Ross created the stunning front cover, which captured everything I wanted and more. My thanks too to Colin Wood, for proofreading, and to Grażyna Martins for typesetting. To Áine Ryan in the marketing team and the entire sales department. I must also thank Andrew James for first reaching out, and then introducing me to his exceptional colleagues. Thank you to Rabeeah Moeen at Hachette UK and all those involved with creating the audiobook. Finally, to everyone at JKP who has played a part in making this book a reality, thank you.

Thank you also to Kirsty Howarth, who carried out a thorough legal read of this book.

Finally, thank *you*. Picking up this book is not only a vote of confidence in my writing, which is incredibly kind, but a commitment to learning more about a niche subject and the wider existential themes it encapsulates – whether you're autistic or not. Thank you for your time, and more importantly, your attention, which this subject so desperately needs.

Author's note

To reflect the terminology adopted by those interviewed for this book, the word "racialized" is used to refer to those from the global majority.

While person-first language is more common on an international level, this book adopts identity-first language to reflect the social model of disability, which is supported by many disabled people in the UK, where the author is based.

INTRODUCTION

T rust breaks in the most unusual way. It's unlike anything materialistic, in that there isn't a repair shop for damaged relationships, and no glue will bridge the gap between the two parties.

Its split is noticeable. When it happens to a community instead of just one individual, the apprehension continues for generations. The animosity expands at a pace with which it is impossible for the perpetrator to catch up. An idea, once embedded, is much harder to shift. A well-constructed narrative outgrows its creator, and therefore belongs to no one.

Critics will likely dismiss this as merely groupthink, but for marginalized communities, it's a survival tactic. Their identities, history and background – often erased or minimized by those with authority – are safer in the minds of the people: indestructible, ageless and protected. To know who to trust is to know around whom it is safe to be vulnerable. If misplaced, then such vulnerability paves the way to exploitation. Trust, so often wedded to and dependent upon the truth, paves the way to dishonesty when broken.

Yet truth, once understood through a collectively agreed definition, now means different things to different people. The politically tumultuous year of 2016 saw honesty weaponized by those in positions of power. Truth became a commodity. In the US, a reality star turned politician was silencing scrutiny from the press – an industry subservient to the truth – as "fake news". Across the pond, buses were emblazoned with misleading figures about how much money the UK could save to fund its National Health Service if it left the European Union. "The people of this country have had enough," then Justice Secretary Michael Gove MP told Sky News' Faizal Islam, "of experts from organizations with acronyms saying they know what is best and getting it consistently wrong."

Though for the autistic community, on which this book focuses, a devastating decline in trust of experts – more specifically, non-autistic or neurotypical researchers studying autism – occurred long before 2016. The *how* will be explored later, but a collective truth had been adopted by a community often associated with a heightened sense of morality: allistic (that is, non-autistic) academics are not to be trusted – a view researchers are still trying to dismantle at the time of writing.

It would be inaccurate to claim trust issues only concern autism researchers within the wider disability community, however. Russian scientist Denis Rebrikov received international condemnation – not least from Deaf communities across the globe – in 2019, when it was reported that he wanted to use the gene editing tool CRISPR to eradicate a mutation which caused deafness in babies.

Meanwhile, the US's National Institute on Aging reported in 2020 that according to estimates, 50% or more of adults with Down's syndrome will develop dementia as a result of Alzheimer's disease. Despite this, a paper from American academics Alldred et al. in October 2021 claimed that out of "hundreds" of trials for treatments for Alzheimer's listed on the international clinicaltrials.gov database, fewer than ten involved those with Down's syndrome.

All of this is to say that while autism research is the focus of this book, other disabilities have too been affected by medical ableism and by approaches and practices that have undertones of eugenics. The conversations around legitimate research that truly benefits marginalized groups, explored in the following pages and chapters, aren't exclusive to the autistic community.

To go one further: building trust, having constructive dialogues and communicating better are themes that appeal to every single one of us. It is hoped that everyone stands to learn something from this book's findings.

Though there is, of course, nuance surrounding these aforementioned issues, and so to simply place the blame on ableism and ways of thinking that can lead all too quickly to eugenics-style thinking would be a great oversimplification of the problem, and make for a very short inquiry. Equally, research can be and is beneficial to the autistic community – especially when it's carried out by autistic people themselves.

When done right, autism research can suggest practices to improve health outcomes for autistic people, and help quantify their lived experiences. It has the power to showcase what is arguably one of the most fascinating aspects of the autistic community and, indeed, the wider disability community: individuality within the commonality. Essentially, that autism (and, by extension, disability) shapes the lives of each person in its own unique way, but they can find community and companionship amongst shared traits and experiences. It's the seemingly contradictory idea that we are united by a disability, identity or condition – but one that affects us all differently.

As for why this book takes a closer look at autism research in particular, the answer lies in what I was doing in the months leading up to writing this.

I had spent a significant amount of time investigating the UK government's failure to provide an in-person sign language interpreter for its coronavirus briefings. A judicial review, brought by one Katie Rowley, would go on to find the Cabinet Office in breach of equality legislation in two instances. I was now looking for a new controversy to examine.

It emerged at a time when I was yet to be diagnosed as autistic myself. In the UK, autistic advocates were speaking out against a research project run by the University of Cambridge, known as Spectrum 10K.

Far from being a charity fun run – as the name seems to suggest – the study was soon shrouded in controversy, and I wanted to find out why. A selection of my discoveries are shared later in this book, with the full investigation available on my website, liamodell.com.

A few months after I received my autism diagnosis in September 2021, I soon learned the problem wasn't exclusive to the UK. The US has its SPARK (Simons Foundation Powering Autism Research for Knowledge) study and the rest of Europe has the GEMMA (Genome, Environment, Microbiome and Metabolome in Autism) project funded by the European Commission. Three of the biggest autism research initiatives in the world right now, and each one has been met with contention.

Their emergence in recent years is just one of the reasons why I started this book, but there is, of course, the far more serious and pressing issue of distrust – one that will only continue if the current problems with autism research go unaddressed.

Impactful research for this community, many would argue, includes the *involvement* of said community, but how can that occur if they are untrusting of academics? Equally, how can non-autistic researchers make recommendations when they are not autistic themselves, or worse yet, haven't co-authored their study with the group concerned? A failure to answer these urgent questions now risks autistic people becoming more distanced from research about them, and allistic academics shaping more of the narrative about autism which belongs to autistic people. The potential impact is of concern on both a practical and ideological level, affecting both sides of the divide.

It would therefore be misguided to only frame these problems as belonging to – or being caused by – autism researchers. The nuance is complex, but will be broken down across the following pages. This book asks why trust in autism research is so low, where are things going wrong, and perhaps most importantly: how can both communities put it right?

Chapter 1

IN THE WAKE OF WAKEFIELD

It started with a prick. A jab to vaccinate its recipient against measles, mumps and rubella (MMR), once appropriated by a now disgraced doctor, almost delivered a knockout blow to the autistic community. His unsubstantiated suggestion, in an article in *The Lancet* in 1998, was that the MMR vaccine, delivered to children in two doses (at 12 months and three years and four months), might cause autism. More specifically, the former health professional claimed he had discovered "a chronic enterocolitis in children that may be related to neuropsychiatric dysfunction", backed up by an argument that 9 of the 12 vaccinated children he studied were autistic.

Such a suggestion by Andrew Wakefield – then a doctor at the Royal Free Hospital in London – was not only flawed, but decimated vaccine uptake. A total of 88.3% of children in England received the first jab by their second birthday in 1998/99, according to NHS data. By 2003/04, a continuous year-on-year decline meant it had slumped to 79.9%.[1]

The most promising development came in the 2016–17 reporting year, when exactly 95% of children had their first dose of MMR by their fifth birthday and the UK met the World

---

1   NHS Digital (2022).

Health Organization's vaccination target.[2] Then the corona-virus pandemic happened, and the anti-vaccine movement reignited around a jab for COVID-19. The UK's NHS and Health Security Agency launched a new immunization drive for MMR in February 2022, as a "significant drop" in its uptake to its lowest level in a decade sparked concern amongst health professionals.[3]

In an accompanying survey of 2,000 parents of children under five, a third of parents who expressed concerns about the MMR vaccine said it was because they were worried about side-effects. The scepticism elevated by Wakefield decades prior was still alive and well.

While MMR vaccination rates were declining post-Wakefield's paper, autism diagnoses were – according to one heavily cited report from Exeter academics Russell et al. – on the rise. Drawing upon data from the Clinical Practice Research Datalink (CPRD) database, which collects anonymized primary care data in the UK, 3,072 autism diagnoses were recorded in the CPRD in 1998. By 2018, the figure was 65,665.

This increase was occurring as the medical industry was continuing to understand and define autism as a condition. The foundations were set by Austrian physician Hans Asperger – the subgroup's namesake – in his 1944 paper on "autistic psychopathy in childhood", in which a distinction is made between those with "considerable intellectual retardation in addition to autism" and "intellectually intact autistic individuals".

In the document, which was translated into English by Uta Frith and republished in 1991, Asperger said: "This disturbance results in severe and characteristic difficulties of social integration. In many cases the social problems are so profound that they overshadow everything else. In some cases, however, the

---

2   NHS Digital (2017).

3   UK Health Security Agency (2022).

problems are compensated by a high level of original thought and experience."

Just one year before Asperger, fellow Austrian Leo Kanner shared his thoughts on autism, distinguishing between the condition and childhood schizophrenia. He coined the term "extreme autistic loneliness" to describe a focus on the self which "disregards, ignores, shuts out anything that comes to the child from the outside" as inconsequential or overwhelming. There also was a "powerful desire" for "sameness" which, along with the loneliness, was "inborn" and "[came] into the world" with them.

Kanner's 1943 paper also included the claim that "there are very few really warmhearted fathers and mothers" within the group he observed, and that "the question arises" as to "whether or what extent" parental issues "contributed to the condition of the children".

A comment attributed to Kanner in an article for *TIME* from 1948 saw him adopt the metaphor that autistic children were "kept neatly in a refrigerator which didn't defrost", a remark that formed part of the so-called "refrigerator mother" theory which falsely blamed "cold" parents for their child's autism.

He is also widely understood to have come up with the phrase "early infantile autism".

Almost two decades prior to Kanner and Asperger, though, was Grunya Sukhareva. A Ukrainian-born child psychiatrist, she coined the term "schizoid psychopathy" around 1925 when she observed six boys in Moscow. According to Swedish researchers Irina Manouilenko and Susanne Bejerot's 2015 study of Sukhareva's work, one of the subheadings in the child psychiatrist's paper details what she called an "autistic attitude" – essentially, a "tendency towards solitude and avoidance of other people from early childhood onwards", with those exhibiting such an attitude "[avoiding] company with other children".

A more significant moment, however, happened in 1980. The

third edition of the *Diagnostic and Statistical Manual of Mental Disorders* (DSM-III), from the American Psychiatric Association, followed on from diagnostic criteria set by UK psychiatrist Michael Ritter and established six requirements for a diagnosis of "infantile autism". These were that traits were onset before the individual was 30 months old; there was a "pervasive lack of responsiveness" to others; language development deficits; "peculiar" speech, if the individual could speak; "bizarre" responses to environmental stimuli; and a lack of delusions and hallucinations associated with schizophrenia.

The concept of an autism spectrum, meanwhile, is credited to UK researcher Lorna Wing. In 1979, together with fellow academic Judith Gould, she questioned the sub-grouping of "typical" autism, writing that "studying only Kanner's syndrome or some other subgroup [...] will lead to conclusions of limited generalisability". The paper also cited three impairments that would later become known as the "triad of impairments": a lack of social interaction, communication and imagination. Wing was also the one to introduce Asperger's syndrome to an English-speaking audience in 1981 (prior to Wing's 1991 translation), with the publication of her paper 'Asperger's syndrome: A clinical account'.

The next volume of the DSM came in 1994, four years before Wakefield et al.'s 1998 *Lancet* paper, and described autistic disorder as an "abnormal or impaired development in social interaction and communication and a markedly restricted repertoire of activity and interests". It was one of five conditions listed under pervasive developmental disorders, which also included atypical autism, Rett's disorder and Asperger's disorder – the latter of which was made distinct from autistic disorder "by the lack of delay in language development". It would only be diagnosed if an individual did not meet the criteria for the other condition.

By 2013, the DSM-5 subsumed all of these into a single "autism spectrum disorder", concerning impaired social interaction and repetitive behaviour, interests or activities all present from childhood. It was, in that respect, ahead of its time, as a 2018 study from Herwig Czech of the Medical University of Vienna unearthed Hans Asperger's links to Nazism and found the researcher "publicly legitimized race hygiene policies including forced sterilizations and, on several occasions, actively cooperated with the child 'euthanasia' program". The revelation led to many in the autistic community distancing themselves from the diagnostic label.

The DSM's international counterpart, the World Health Organization's International Classification of Diseases (ICD), only took the same step in establishing an "autism spectrum disorder" as recently as 2019, in its 11th revision, which came into effect in February 2022.

Though back in 1998, it's likely the ongoing medicalization of autism – and its deficit-based focus on what individuals with a diagnosis could *not* do, rather than how differently they perceived the world around them – led to parents taking a more fatalistic view of autism in relation to their child or children. The fall in MMR vaccinations was alarming, and for some parents, fuelled by their ableist view that they would rather have a child at risk of exposure to deadly diseases than an autistic one.

In addition to a sample of 12 children – who received lumbar (spinal) punctures and a rectal examination known as an ileocolonoscopy – being far from representative, a significant flaw was present right in the text itself. The suggestion of a link between the MMR vaccine and autism, although unfounded, was enough to plant doubt in the minds of new parents, and there was plenty of evidence unearthed by British investigative journalist Brian Deer to suggest Wakefield wanted that to happen. One clinician's letter – quoted in Deer's incisive book on the matter from 2020, *The Doctor Who Fooled the World* – set out the psychology at play when it came to one parent of a young, autistic child: "She is very sad and is looking both for somebody or something to blame and also for specific treatments for [her son], and I'm afraid I have not been able to help her on either count."

Deer went on to explain the binary choice or "trap" that faced those who paid attention to Wakefield's nonsense: they could choose to go down a path of pity, or they could "accuse someone else". There had to be someone to blame. There had to be a cause.

The vaccine and its use as a supposed origin of a child's autism was perfect: so abstract in its explanation that a parent's story could be adapted to fit Wakefield's mould. Like psychic mediumship, the doctor had thrown an idea out into the crowd, and those who would listen had to work to make it make sense. Deer called it a "feedback loop of confirmation". Parents, he said, heard Wakefield's arguments and "interpreted their children's histories in that light."

Even if medical professionals were trying to reinforce solidified science and research on MMR and autism to sceptical parents, the parents didn't trust them. It came back to a concern that both the Department of Health and general practitioners (GPs) had vested interests. As one member of a focus group, which took place between November 2002 and March 2003, told Glasgow academics: "What do you do as a parent? You don't know who to trust." The mother, who has an autistic child, continued: "You're meant to trust your doctor implicitly and yet people are saying, 'well, you know, they're getting paid for having so many people vaccinated and all this', and you start thinking, 'well... who's got my wee boy's best interests at heart?'"[4] She was referring to immunization target payments, which saw GP practices paid a sum for each jab delivered. Clearly, some parents interpreted this as monetizing healthcare, placing the prospect of extra income for cash-strapped services above healthcare

---

4   Hilton, Petticrew and Hunt (2007).

decisions – decisions which should be person-specific, and free from financial influence.

Concerns around the economic interests in healthcare – and indeed autism research – remain an issue of contention to this day, as later chapters will make clear.

But that didn't happen with Wakefield. Against the institutional narratives of healthcare workers, politicians and more, he was but one man offering a different take on the vaccine narrative. The election of Donald Trump as president of the United States and the UK's decision to leave the European Union were seen as the collapse of a prevailing establishment rhetoric. The "post-truth" era, it was called, but Wakefield had got there sooner. "Here were campaigners who grasped the paradox of the age [of Trump and Brexit]," wrote Deer, "that the more incredible and outlandish their claims, the more these might be spread and believed."

The lack of clear guidance for parents post-diagnosis didn't help matters. As Steve Silberman wrote in his book *Neurotribes*, "Parents of children born in the last decade of the twentieth century had to make their way forward through a maze of conflicting information. Was autism a congenital and incurable developmental disorder rooted in the complexities of the human genome, or a toxic by-product of a corrupt medical establishment driven to seek profit at all costs?"

There was a gap in knowledge and a loss of trust in those in positions of authority. Wakefield's hypothesis on the MMR vaccine, so unsubstantiated in nature, filled the vacuum.

"Our own [study] would support the hypothesis that the consequences of an inflamed or dysfunctional intestine may play a part in behavioural changes in some children," Wakefield et al. wrote in the retracted *Lancet* paper. It would go on to borrow from "the 'opioid excess' theory of autism" previously proposed by several academics such as Jaak Panksepp, Karl Reichelt and Paul Shattock. It argues, in Wakefield's interpretation, that autism occurs as a result of "the incomplete breakdown and excessive absorption of gut-derived peptides from foods", peptides being amino acids, and the examples of food given being barley, oats and rye. Wakefield and colleagues, applying the opioid excess theory, believed these peptides may affect "central nervous system opioids" and thus could lead to the "disruption of normal neuroregulation and brain development".

Then came the *nudge, nudge, wink, wink* of a suggestion that autism came from the MMR vaccine. "We have identified a chronic enterocolitis in children that may be related to neuropsychiatric dysfunction," concluded Wakefield and his colleagues. "In most cases, onset of symptoms was after measles, mumps and rubella immunisation. Further investigations are needed to examine this syndrome and its possible relation to this vaccine."

Deer, as is to be expected, offered a better summary of the above in his book: "Persistent measles virus led to bowel inflammation. Then an 'excess' of peptides from food escaped into the bloodstream, travelled to the brain, and caused damage."

Rather frustratingly, Wakefield's focus on the gut in relation to autism is not entirely misplaced. Studies far more rigorous than the disgraced doctor's 12-parent project attest to autistic people being more likely to have an inflammatory bowel disease (IBD) such as ulcerative colitis or Crohn's disease. The latter of these two conditions had also been studied by Wakefield.

A 2014 paper from McElhanon, McCracken, Karpen and Sharp at Emory University School of Medicine in Atlanta, Georgia – in which they analysed 15 studies – found "children with [autism spectrum disorder] experience significantly more GI [gastrointestinal] symptoms than comparison groups".

A year later, academics from Massachusetts, Connecticut and North Carolina published a report in the *Inflammatory Bowel Diseases* journal in which they concluded that "across each population with different kinds of ascertainment, there was a consistent and statistically significant increased prevalence of IBD in patients with ASD [autism spectrum disorder] than their respective controls and nationally reported rates for paediatric IBD".[5] Then, in 2018, researchers at the Uniformed Services University of the Health Sciences in Maryland found children diagnosed with ASD were "more likely to meet [the] criteria" for Crohn's and ulcerative colitis than controls.[6]

More recently, in July 2023, a group of European researchers claimed to have produced the first study to "identify a genetic link between the GI tract and ASD".[7]

Gut issues in autistic people are, undoubtedly, well evidenced. Wakefield's speculation about vaccines causing autism were quite the opposite. Nevertheless, soon came the panic – a moral panic, without question.

Moral panic is a phenomenon defined by Oxford Reference as "a mass movement based on the false or exaggerated perception that some cultural behaviour or group of people is dangerously deviant and poses a threat to society's values and interests. Moral panics are generally fuelled by media coverage of social issues." The movement – specifically the anti-vaccine movement – had always been lurking, but it mobilized around Wakefield, emboldened by a careless media, politicians and others in high-profile positions.

England's chief medical officer at the time, Sir Kenneth Caiman, requested the Medical Research Council (MRC) conduct an "independent scientific seminar" to review Wakefield's work – which it did on 23 March 1998 – and found no evidence to suggest a causal link between the MMR vaccine and autism.[8] Yet, the optics were there for everyone to see. The fact that a

5   Doshi-Velez et al. (2015).
6   Lee et al. (2018).
7   Lombardi et al. (2023).
8   Laurance (1998).

body as official as the MRC had to investigate suggested there may well have been *some* credibility to Wakefield's claims – even when it would soon transpire that there wasn't.

The press didn't help, either. One *Daily Mirror* report from 1998 was clear in the picture it wanted to paint. A young girl, beaming wide for a photograph in a red dress. Then, the caption underneath: "Lost smile: Melissa was a happy little girl before she was vaccinated."[9] It was ominous. The vaccine and its supposed "triggering" of autism had made a young girl emotionless – such was the implication. The "othering" was chilling, presenting it as a virus or disease inflicted upon a person, rather than a neurological condition. Parents believed there was the "child of pre-MMR" somewhere in there, now concealed by autism as if it were some kind of accessory, instead of something that was always there, waiting to be identified and diagnosed.

A BBC News headline at the time, meanwhile, failed to tell the full story.[10] It said the MMR vaccine was "linked to autism", giving credence when there wasn't any, and citing only the "raised alarms" from Wakefield in his paper which hadn't been replicated. He was advocating for the three-in-one MMR to be delivered in three separate doses, the BBC also reported – a fitting recommendation when Deer would later reveal in his 2020 book that Wakefield was looking into patents for single-dose vaccines. Wakefield's aims and talking points were being parroted uncritically by Britain's mainstream media.

This was foreshadowing a dilemma raised by Vote Leave's infamous red bus in the 2016 EU referendum: what could the media do if a prominent source was parroting falsehoods? Wakefield's idea was out there, helped by the media and groups of parents concerned about vaccines and their impact on their children – JABS (Justice, Awareness and Basic Support) being

---

9   *The Mirror* (1998).
10   BBC News (1998).

the most prominent. Jackie Fletcher is one of its figureheads, who was involved in the origin of the pressure group after her son Robert had the MMR jab as a one-year-old and was later diagnosed with epilepsy.

"Ten days later he started convulsing," Mrs Fletcher told *The Independent* in 1994, four years before Wakefield's *Lancet* paper was published. "We went by ambulance to the Royal Albert Edward Infirmary, Wigan [...] Our son was eventually diagnosed as epileptic as well as having a very rare acquired immunodeficiency problem."[11]

In May 2010, the General Medical Council (GMC) decided to strike Wakefield off the medical register, criticizing a "breach of trust of patients and employers" when he ordered investigations on children, despite having no paediatric qualifications; the repeated breaches of "fundamental principles of research medicine"; and the "callous disregard for any distress or pain" children might suffer as a result of Wakefield collecting samples of their blood for research. These samples were collected at a birthday party in exchange for £5 – behaviour the GMC said "brought the profession into disrepute".

Unsurprisingly, the Council found Wakefield guilty of "serious professional misconduct" and that erasure from the register was the most appropriate sanction "to protect patients" and ensure "the maintenance of public trust and confidence in the profession", and the only one proportionate to the "serious and wide-ranging findings" made against him.

It was right for the GMC to be so serious in their ruling. What is arguably the most high-profile study into autism led to a misplaced and widespread belief in vaccine damage. As for the level of trust in the profession, the autistic community has become even more sceptical of autism research since. Questions around the causality and biology of the condition still linger in

---

11   Roberts (1994).

the research space, and while there are legitimate reasons for investigating autism on a genetic level (as later chapters will explain), the fear of it being the beginning of a slippery slope to eugenics or other harmful practices remains.

In other words, autism had already been at the centre of an academic scandal, and the community did not want to see it happen again. They would have to fight to reclaim the narrative around their own condition, and it wouldn't be easy. A complete move away from genetic and biomedical research into autism would be ill-advised and counter-productive – not least when it comes to investigating co-occurring and co-morbid conditions such as attention deficit hyperactivity disorder (ADHD) and the connective tissue disorder known as Ehlers-Danlos syndrome (EDS).

Not only that, but for some, participating in genetic research into autism would yield some significant results.

Chapter 2

THE RIGHT TO KNOW

"It was very strange to suddenly be thrust into that world," autistic sexuality advocate and public speaker Amy Gravino tells me over Zoom, her choice of background being – I'm told – *The Birth of Venus* by Sandro Botticelli. "It changed everything and it changed nothing at the same time."

In 2016, she volunteered a sample to the SPARK study, a project looking to "advance the understanding of autism" and its "genetic basis", as well as "improve the lives" of autistic people by "identifying the causes of autism". The project lists the controversial US organization Autism Speaks as one of its community partners. She wasn't expecting to receive any kind of result, but she got one, five years later.

Gravino was told she had Kleefstra syndrome, a rare genetic condition "characterized by intellectual disability" caused predominantly by a missing piece or "deletion" of the ninth chromosome, with links to autism.[1]

"I guess what made me anxious was feeling that what I believed about my disability – my autism – could that no longer be true?" she explains. "I had a little bit of an identity crisis at that moment. I think I cried, actually, when I read it. Like, I flat-out

---

1   KleefstraSyndrome.org (2017).

sobbed reading it, because it was kind of a shock, but I know where I come from. I know that I'm my father's daughter, and that doesn't change with this information."

So why would someone seek out genetic information about their autism if it would only serve to confirm what they already knew?

"It may not have had a huge impact for me, but that doesn't mean it can't be important for someone else," she responds, "someone who is experiencing co-occurring conditions, medical conditions that are seriously inhibiting their quality of life, that are affecting their ability to have adaptive skills and be part of society.

"I understand the fears that many autistic people have," adds Gravino, before saying, "People, far too often, leap to the whole eugenics thing.

"I'm very tired of seeing that word, because I feel like it's been stripped of so much meaning when we throw it around just so frequently, and we don't look at what that really means. If we're saying that genetic testing is eugenics, we're ignoring that it's multifaceted.

"This is not about eliminating autistic people," she stresses. "This is about potentially identifying the causes, the root behind these medical issues that are really causing people physical harm and pain. People get really alarmed and I understand that. I get why people get so freaked out and why there is that reaction, but for a lot of folks, they're kind of only seeing it within the scope of their own experience.

"They're not seeing these other people's experiences and seeing that just because this is not the case for you, there are other people who are – I try not to use this word, but – suffering," says Gravino. "Some people are suffering from medical issues that really are damaging them, so I would not want to withhold something that could be life-changing for someone else, just because it wasn't that for me."

The distinction between meaningful medical research into autism – be it the co-occurring conditions or traits which could be treated in some way – and studies that risk paving the way to the detailed make-up of the condition (and therefore, fears of a cure) is not exactly straightforward. A commitment not to contribute to eugenics or 'curing' autism, it seems, is no longer enough.

I ask Gravino how autistic individuals can trust that the biomedical research in which they participate doesn't lead to such a troubling outcome, and what's needed from researchers to reassure them.

"It's important to research and find out information about the organizations who are behind this research," she replies. "Find out: have they integrated autistic people into the research design, have they collaborated with autistic researchers or folks on the spectrum – not just as participants in the studies, but as co-investigators? How invested are they in supporting neuro-diversity and things like that?"

Gravino gives the example of SPARK, to which she has not only volunteered her genetic data, but also her time as a scientific advisory board member. Its website sets out the various boards, councils and committees overseeing its work. The Scientific Advisory Board issues guidance and influences the study's research agenda. Its Community Advisory Council "ensures the voice of [the] community" is represented in their research. The Diversity, Equity and Inclusion Advisory Board, the purpose of which is rather self-explanatory, looks to "increase representation of communities of colour in autism research". Lastly, the Participant Access Committee reviews applications from autism research studies looking to connect with "qualified members of the SPARK community".

With any research study, Gravino says communication is paramount. "There has to be clear, explicit communication from the researchers, and there has to be clear communication from the autistic individual," she explains. "Dialogue can be challenging for some folks, but if there is a willingness to collaborate, then the researchers will be willing to find a way to have the autistic people communicate in whatever way works for them.

"It doesn't have to be verbal," she clarifies, "it could be written, it could be whatever it might be. But all too often, there's a breakdown in that communication and people just get defensive and it shuts everything down. We don't have these moderate discussions.

"I've had to stop engaging on Twitter [since rebranded to X] because I'm just going to put my head through a wall. I mean, not literally, hopefully, but I can't deal with it."

Social media is a subject that provokes an emotional response from Gravino. She has a masters degree in the controversial topic of applied behavioural analysis (ABA), a "treatment" for autism which is commonly seen as problematic due to its emphasis on rewarding actions that more closely align with neurotypical behaviourism, and discouraging those that don't – for example, the autistic processing technique known as stimming.

It's a practice condemned by many autistic advocates and explored in further detail in Chapter 8. One of its early pioneers, Ole Ivar Lovaas, used the reward and punishment model in one 1974 study into "deviant sex-role behaviours" in male children, which essentially amounted to gay conversion therapy.

ABA is a contentious issue, but Gravino's comments about the toxicity of social media sites such as Twitter and their failure to foster civilized discussions seem far less controversial.

"I've been called a traitor. I've been called way worse than that on Twitter," she says, her voice wavering. "I've cried from the things that I've been called because this is the community that I'm trying to help and be part of, and it is very painful and upsetting to have horrific things said about you.

"I've had to develop a thicker skin but I could take it when it comes from a lot of other directions," continues Gravino. "I don't really care what people think of me, but there's something about when it comes from a fellow autistic person that cuts through my heart. It really does."

The advocate's comments tie into her remarks about medical studies reassuring people. "I think everybody here is trying to do a good thing, is trying to make a difference in people's lives, but we are not listening to each other," she tells me. "We're not listening, and then that's really what causes this to just hit this stalemate.

"Because when this explodes on social media, then the concern becomes PR, and how do we mitigate this from being a PR disaster?" explains Gravino, adding that it isn't just about PR but "tangible change".

"That's part of influencing the culture of research: how do we make this something that is actually visible? The people I know who are like moderates who are able to see both sides and want to communicate, they're not on social media, because we're out there in the world trying to do this stuff," she continues. "We don't have time to yell on social media, and so the folks on [there] are kind of a minority.

"They're a very, very vocal minority, I think in that, but they become representative of the community as a whole, which I think creates a problem, because then researchers get this impression that this is what the autistic community is, and they don't want to engage.

"I'm not saying it's our job to be palatable and presentable and to do all the heavy lifting," stresses Gravino, "it obviously needs to be meeting halfway – but we have to know that this is causing more harm than good, I think, in the long run."

There are, of course, legitimate cases for being interested in medical research into autism. "In terms of why we are more likely to have epilepsy," says autistic content creator Bodhrán Mullan as one example. "I'm also interested in why do we stim?

Why do our brains interpret things as being more or less? Why are we dialled differently in terms of the brain? How does that work? I'm fascinated to know what makes that happen, but too many times it's 'we need to find the root cause'."

"I think there's a temptation to trash all biomedical-based autism research," argues Fergus Murray, an autistic writer and teacher, "and I think it's understandable, but it's probably a mistake. It leads us into some very difficult territory because, for example, research on the causes of EDS and potential treatments for [it] – given the very high overlap between EDS, hypermobility and neurodivergence – is likely to lead to potential treatment or prevention of autism in some sense.

"It's completely possible that drugs which would change the collagen system in such a way that people no longer have terrible EDS pain will turn out to make people less monotropic – 'less autistic'."

Vicki Wistow, an autistic Twitter user, sums it up perfectly in one tweet: "Knowledge is knowing autism is genetic. Wisdom is knowing that humanity can't be trusted to know which genes it is."

Autistic people should not be deprived of the right to explore their DNA, but there is a conflict at play: allowing for genuine investigations into co-morbid conditions, while at the same time ensuring it doesn't pave the way to eradicating autism.

"There are lots of co-occurring conditions, physical conditions, that really impact the wellbeing of autistic people," explains Dr Heini Natri, an autistic computational biologist at Arizona's Translational Genomics Research Institute. "It's important to think about how we can do this biomedical and genetics research to address some of those issues in a way that is safe, and respects the autonomy and individual's rights.

"There are some important questions about, for example, biobanking and building databases that include genetic information and other information on autistic people, or any vulnerable population, really," she continues. "These are questions that people are thinking about in the field of genetics more widely, not just in the context of autism research, but other marginalized or vulnerable communities.

"There really are no good answers as to how to do that," admits Dr Natri. "What happens all the time is that the technology develops faster than we're able to develop ethical guidelines to prevent the misuse or violations in the use of that kind of information."

Such guidelines are already being considered by researchers, with Dr Natri making the case for an ethical framework for genetic autism research in a paper in press at the time of writing.[2]

"Specific concerns range from lack of benefit to future data use and privacy, increased discrimination, and the possibility that data or study results will be used in prevention," she writes. In her view, a framework is necessary to address a string of concerns, and has been suggested by advocacy groups such as the Autistic Self Advocacy Network (ASAN).

"Recent lapses have revealed ethical gaps and a lack of sufficient engagement and inclusion in genetic and biomedical autism research, demonstrating that existing practices, ethical guidelines, regulations and review processes are inadequate," she continues. "Many of the outstanding ethical issues in autism genetics are the same core issues identified in genetic research on other marginalized communities: researchers' repeated failures to engage communities in ethical and inclusive ways, lack of transparency, and historical and recent abuses all have contributed to distrust between researchers and the key stakeholders."

The criteria within such a framework will continue to be discussed, but Dr Natri has some ideas. "Specific consideration will be given to recommendations to address power imbalances,

---

2   Natri (n.d.).

for building trust through transparency and accountability, and ensuring safety, autonomy and research benefits to autistic people," she writes. "Wide-ranging and practical recommendations will be made regarding socially responsible research; autistic inclusion, participatory research, and ethical engagement with the autistic community; dissemination of research findings; and guarding against violations and harm."

One way in which harm can be prevented, suggests Dr Natri, is by those in the field of genetics acknowledging "current and past malpractice and its impact on marginalized, vulnerable communities".

Just how easy it will be for genetic researchers to accept such a thing, however, is another matter. "I think it's very difficult for individuals to acknowledge that something that they contributed to could be harmful," Dr Natri tells me over Zoom. "No one wants to do that, which is understandable.

"So I think the pressure has to come from institutions – from funding agencies, research agencies like [the National Institutes of Health], and so on. That can really help shift things."

She also, like Gravino, points out how Twitter influences autism research and communication. "When autism researchers are communicating some of their studies or findings on [the platform], for example, I'm sure you notice sometimes, [...] these kind of situations where an autism researcher is talking about their research and dozens or hundreds of autistic people are reacting really negatively to that."

She continues. "It's an interesting situation because it's clear that a lot of autism researchers are not aware of what is happening in the autistic community," she says, "then it comes to them as a surprise that what they're doing is not really what the autistic community wants or needs, or the problems in their work are not obvious to them, clearly. It didn't occur to them that there might be this negative response."

Another realization is occurring in the industry too. "One

of the things that my field is now starting to talk more about and acknowledge is that most problems that members of marginalized communities face do not have a biological remedy," explains Dr Natri. "Most problems that autistic people have do not have a biomedical or genetic solution, and probably never will.

"It's complicated because there are these legitimate medical, physical and mental problems and autistic people do want there to be interventions or remedies or solutions to those problems," she goes on to add. "It's important to say those things, but at the same time, you need to consider the other factors. It's just as important, if not more important, to consider the societal factors."

Safe genetic and biomedical research, argues Dr Natri, considers how societal and cultural factors influence the type of work academics do. "The whole reason why most of autism research is really focused on the causes, and making autistic people less autistic, is the societal reasons," she says. "The negative bias – autistic people are perceived negatively – that is the reason. That continues to influence and direct the type of research that is done and the type of conclusions that people are drawing from their studies."

There is a split between research into medical and social issues, but can they operate in harmony?

"In some respects, I think they have to," answers Liz Pellicano, a non-autistic autism researcher and professor of autism research at University College London, "because we're kind of stuck with the DSM and the ICD, and those routes to diagnosis allow people to get some services where they are available, and support. I think in an ideal world, we would have a system where we wouldn't necessarily need a diagnosis. We would kind of acknowledge that people have different ways of being in the world and doing, and that sometimes – as we all do – we need some support with those things, and so we would identify that level of need or support on an individual level, but I think we're far away from doing that.

"The medical model paints an excessively narrow view of autism," she continues. "It's very deficit-based and it also has very little focus on the context in which people live (whether that's within school, at home, at work and in the community) and that's what I think the social model does really well – focusing on those contextual aspects."

The neurodiversity paradigm – which, along with the social model, is examined in more detail later in this book – is brought up by Dr Kristen Bottema-Beutel, a non-autistic associate professor of special education at Boston College, when I ask her a similar question about harmonizing medical and social model research. "I think that's what neurodiversity scholars are trying to do," she says. "I think that the neurodiversity paradigm clearly comes from the social model, but I don't think that it rejects everything about the medical model. I think that really innovative scholarship in that part of autism research is happening because autistic people are leading it.

"I think they are doing really complex and innovative work to see what from those two models needs to be kept together and unified."

Zachary Williams, co-chair of the Autistic Researchers Committee within the International Society for Autism Research (INSAR), shares a different take. "I feel like at least some of the end goals of the biomedical research are really just knowledge for knowledge's sake," he says. "I think that, in some cases, people are worried about the looming spectre of biomedical treatments that will wipe out autism and I'm very unconvinced by a lot of those arguments. Look at all of the biological psychiatry research that's gone into every other psychiatric condition in history. It's definitely not done a very good job at wiping any of those out.

"I think we're pretty safe here to say that autism is here

to stay and we'll be OK," continues Williams. "It's probably unlikely that basic science is going to cure autism and we will probably just waste money on it rather than threaten autistic people's livelihoods."

Of course, as has been made clear in comments already featured in this chapter, some autistic people *do* have the desire to know more about autism through genetic research. Equally, when these studies involve public bodies such as universities and NHS trusts, it becomes a case of the British public having a *right* to know.

The right was granted in the UK in 2000 with the Freedom of Information (FOI) Act. Save for a number of exemptions – some of which can be challenged on public interest grounds – individuals can request documentation and correspondence on a particular subject.

The potential of this is significant, unearthing private attitudes held by researchers and academics which they choose not to air publicly. As later chapters will reveal, it has the power to highlight study descriptions and aims which haven't been pushed through a sanitized, PR-focused machine. It can shine a light on meetings and discussions that influence the direction of the study, and ethically questionable research practices.

Data protection laws also offer an avenue for further revelations. Individuals can, in most circumstances, make subject access requests about the details held about them – and amend or request removal of this data. When data is shared, there is parity, and parity is an essential pillar of trust.

Autistic people have a right to know about research concerning their data, or indeed involving their money as taxpayers, when such studies are carried out by public authorities. Whether these academics *want* autistic people to know about – and potentially challenge – their work is another question entirely.

Chapter 3

THE ALLISTIC IRONY

"It's so absurd that just a true and faithful reading of science leads to this. It's an untold story," Andrew Whitehouse, professor of autism research at Telethon Kids and the University of Western Australia, tells the news outlet *Spectrum* (rebranded to *The Transmitter* in December 2023, but referred to throughout this book as *Spectrum* to avoid confusion) in early 2022.[1]

Nevertheless, after co-authoring a report into autism interventions in November 2020, which stated that few came with sufficient research to support them, he went on to claim individuals and organizations were threatening to sue him. Some had complained to his employers, and others allegedly went as far as to harass his family to the extent their safety was at risk.

This isn't the only damning incident of individuals not taking too kindly to the scrutiny of autism research. Dr Monique Botha, an autistic early career research fellow from the University of Stirling, shares their experiences in a frank September 2021 critical reflection titled 'Academic, activist, or advocate? Angry, entangled, and emerging: A critical reflection on autism knowledge production'.

They write that in their last year of studying for their PhD,

---

1 Zamzow (2022).

they submitted a paper containing a section on how autistic people are dehumanized in the research industry, only for one academic to accuse Dr Botha of slander for labelling their work as dehumanizing, and one peer reviewer to suggest they amend the paper to stress not all autism research can be considered as such.

Dr Botha notes they had a BA, MSc and PhD to their name at this point, along with three peer-reviewed papers, but that they still faced accusations of bias. They suggest the issue is less about the literature itself, but rather their being autistic and that autistic people cannot be trusted to talk about their own lived experience.

In July 2022, I received a pre-print copy of a study co-authored by Dr Botha and Dr Eilidh Cage (a non-autistic psychology lecturer, also from the University of Stirling). The findings contained in their November 2022 paper, "'Autism research is in crisis": A mixed method study of researcher's constructions of autistic people and autism research', were just as stark.

They found that out of 195 autism researchers, 60% exhibited ableist cues in the form of either dehumanizing, objectifying or stigmatizing autistic people, which led them to call for a vital shift in the language autism researchers use to discuss this demographic and conduct their studies.

The paper's conclusion acknowledged a link between the involvement of autistic people in research about them and a decreased likelihood of the aforementioned cues of ableism coming up in the narratives used by researchers, but the same publication also detected an apprehension towards autistic people participating in autism research, arguing that their inclusion was considered a threat by non-autistic academics regarding their place in the industry.

One survey respondent even told the academic duo that the field is "in crisis" because established allistic academics are being "pushed out".

Co-author Dr Cage also questioned her own position within the autism research industry as a non-autistic academic, writing that there can be a sense that only a small number of them are adopting a stance that is opposed to ableism, and even that might not be considered sufficient in terms of combating the problem. She pondered whether it is necessary to feel discomfort – and, in fact, share the emotional burden of research with autistic academics – in order to begin the process of understanding the need for change, and encouraged peers to not feel "pushed out" by this feeling, but "pulled in" instead.

There's a lot of ideas explored by autism researchers which autistic people have found hurtful, too, with Dr Botha and Dr Cage writing that autistic people's worth rested on their societal contribution, often confined to two variables: intelligence and independence.

Then there's the autism researchers who responded to Dr Botha and Dr Cage's survey to describe autistic people as exhibiting a certain kind of rigidity; a sense of being cut off from wider society; or a lack of empathy, responsiveness or alertness to social and cultural norms.

The authors claim such perceptions have influenced how autistic people are described within society in both a social and a cultural sense, and it's easy to see how when we look at the representation and understanding of autism in popular culture.

Despite their creators issuing comments which neither confirm nor deny the characters are autistic, Sheldon Cooper of *The Big Bang Theory* and Christopher Boone of Mark Haddon's *The Curious Incident of the Dog in the Night-Time* are still nonetheless perceived as such by a section of viewers and readers respectively. Cooper, played by Jim Parsons in the sitcom, is typically direct and matter-of-fact in his dialogue – a kind of straightforwardness which could easily fall into the negative and reductive label of "rigid". Fifteen-year-old Boone, meanwhile, has a hard time understanding metaphor and often responds literally to what others say to him, despite having many "emotional" moments in the novel due to a difficult family situation. There's a laughable contradiction in affixing the label of a "lack of responsiveness [and] awareness of social cues or cultural norms" to autistic people, while also describing us as "emotional" – often as a result of stimulation we receive from the environments in which we find ourselves.

Some autism researchers' perceptions of autistic people become even more confusing and troubling when it comes to how and when they refer to "autism" versus "autistic people".

Dr Botha and Dr Cage note in their report that the language of prevention was used in relation to autism, but not autistic people, despite autism never existing as an "amorphous" condition because it is always tied to autistic individuals. They argue that such discussion around autism "prevention" is aided by the condition being seen as both a *removed* and a *removable* aspect of an individual's existence.

They go on to add it's possible academics relied on this technique of applying distance through language because the prevention of a condition rather than people comes across as less contentious or controversial, especially when there is abstraction.

Even their attempts to offset such techniques are unsuccessful, as the pair noted some researchers sought to underscore that autistic people are human in order to avoid *dehumanization*, only to disregard the wider community aspects that come with the autistic identity – something which they said also constitutes dehumanization.

Transdisciplinary autistic activist and researcher Dr Moréni-ke Giwa Onaiwu comments: "If you're still prescribing how people need to fit into a box, or what they're allowed to research or what you consider is important, you're defining the objectives. You're defining the needs for people, and then you're expecting them to just rubber stamp it.

"I think another thing is, I think people really don't understand true collaboration," they continue. "Everyone says that they want it, but they don't. They want to bake a cake and they want to throw some icing on the top – that's the community involvement. They want to already have all the ingredients and everything that they need, and this is just a little sweetener on the top. That's not the way it works, because the community needs to be involved from the very beginning. You can't bring someone in at the eleventh hour and ask them to give you feedback in a 30-minute session and think that you're going to be able to make vast improvements.

"You could have [issues] in the conceptualization of something, in the design and the marketing and the wording and a whole bunch of things," she says. "There could be a whole lot of things wrong that you missed, and people say they want to change but they really don't want to change that much. They want to change a little bit. They want to possibly go from maybe lavender to maybe a richer purple, but they don't want to change completely to another colour – but that's often what is needed. We're asking the same questions."

"When I searched academic papers on autism and read opinions written by parents, carers, et cetera of how they viewed autistic people, I was horrified by how we autistics were described/viewed," writes Julianne Higgins, an adjunct associate lecturer at the University of New South Wales, when I ask about any shifts in perspective before and after receiving an autism diagnosis. "Their accounts were not my experience at all, and not my intentions and understanding of my life as an introvert who was always trying to 'do the right thing the right way'. This led me to live as a recluse."

Activist, researcher and speaker Dr TC Waisman – like Higgins – is also a late-diagnosed autistic academic, shares a similar realization. "Once I was diagnosed and had a few years to understand ingrained ableist policies and practices, I took what I knew from the organizational world and applied it to research, higher education, and workplaces," they tell me. "I was astounded at how acceptable it was/is to uphold barriers that shut out those of us with neurological disabilities and how that kind of gatekeeping would be considered cruel if it were applied to those with physical disabilities (which I have as well), but it was and is standard practice for those who are neurodivergent.

"This made me change my trajectory, and though I still coach leaders, I mainly focus on autistic activism and research," she concludes.

This is yet another compelling argument for autistic people having more control over the narrative being told about their disability by autism researchers. From an advocacy perspective, being made to constantly question one's identity at the same time as having to campaign on issues relating to it can be jarring and demoralizing. To put this point across more frankly: how can you confidently advocate for your rights, if you are not made to feel confident in yourself?

It's not too dissimilar from the strain autistic autism researchers experience when studying their own condition. "I ended up in the hospital," reveals Marianthi Kourti, an autistic autism researcher and PhD student at the University of Birmingham. They stress it wasn't the only reason they found themselves in that position, and that their colleagues were wonderful, but it was part of a combination of emotions. Their work on the topic of intimate relationships came at a time they were only just starting to process their own negative experiences in this area.

"I couldn't move away from thinking on one thing and going back to work to just read anybody else's bad experiences and there was very much a pressure of 'my community needs this' I put on myself," they explain. "Then external pressure put on me by the project, because I mean, the community does need this and my colleagues realized that. They were like, 'oh, we need to do the best that we can to make this project as good as possible', which was all well and good and obviously very important, but at the end of the day, they finished work and they went home and they didn't have to think about that any more.

"I finished work, and I still had to wonder like, 'which friend was sexually assaulted now', or 'what are the consequences of me [...] being with this friend' [...], so I never got a break on it."

Dr Tish Marrable, a social care and social work researcher at the University of Sussex, shares her own account of the emotional toll on autistic academics. "I think there can be a problem where allistic [people] – hopefully allies – take the lead on projects," she says. "I was going to put in for a very big project at one point, a couple of years back. I started writing the bid, and then doing all the stuff that you need to do in order to get a bid together like that, because I've had smaller research projects, and I just freaked out, basically.

"I tend to shut down rather than melt down, but I had to walk away from it, basically, because the stress of it was just too overpowering for me. I couldn't do it," she continues. "I do worry that there's this other side of playing the game in academia that may not come easily to autistic people – *some* autistic people, because everybody's different."

Yet at the same time, when talking to autistic autism researchers and advocates, a particular irony leaps out about the behaviour of their non-autistic counterparts. Autistic people have long been described as – and at times, stigmatized for – being averse to change, and yet, when there are calls for non-autistic people (specifically researchers) to do so, *they* are suddenly the ones incapable of adjusting.

"These people don't actually want to face up to the fact that they are the perpetrators," says autistic advocate Maria Scharnke, "and they are doing unethical things and they are hurting children, and that their system is wrong and their system is failing us," she says. "They can't possibly admit to that because how will they live with themselves?

"So they wall themselves in, in all their layers of implausible deniability, and they keep deliberately setting up research and presenting research in a way that suggests that [they are not the ones] at fault, we are the ones that need to change, because that would mean that they change and their methods change, and they are not willing to do that," Scharnke continues. "So as long as they hold the balance of power, they're never ever going to admit to anything that could indict them, and they won't."

I discuss the aforementioned irony with her. "Exactly," she agrees. "I've also noticed that their thinking can be incredibly black and white."

Dr Dave Caudel, an autistic researcher from Vanderbilt University in Tennessee, offers up another trait typically applied to autistic people. "I think so much of this lost trust and such is just miscommunication," he says. "Autistic people are talking to the researchers and the researchers aren't really hearing what they're saying, and when the researchers are talking back, they're not being heard in the way that they think they're being heard. Each person knows what the words mean to them, but they need to make an effort to understand what the words mean to this other person.

"Now, I'm challenging researchers: you have to be more autistic about this," he continues. "You have to recognize that people use language differently, and you have to take that into account when you're trying to communicate with somebody and trying to reach an understanding."

There is the need for consideration, yet there is still a disregard shown towards autistic people by researchers, as Dr Heini Natri explains. "I still think that autistic people are very easily dismissed – members of other marginalized or vulnerable communities are easily dismissed – when they try to advocate for themselves or for each other, but things are definitely changing," she says, "especially now that there are more and more openly autistic researchers and physicians, and other professionals and advocates. We've made a lot of effort to combine our forces and to facilitate this kind of collective action and to write our own papers, create our own institutions and groups. It's easier to have our voices heard when we're working together.

"I feel like for autistic people, it's so easy for others to dismiss us, or the immediate reaction is often a negative reaction," adds Dr Natri. "We do have to work three times as hard to have our voices heard or to be taken seriously, and we have to be very careful not to make mistakes, because if you make a mistake, then someone can very easily dismiss you based on that one mistake."

She too references the protective nature non-autistic researchers have around their legacy, and concerns over shifting paradigms – that is, a set of common beliefs and understandings within the research field. "I feel like you have to be kind of vigilant and it's not necessarily always even safe to be interacting with some non-autistic autism researchers who are very invested and attached to their current model and paradigm, and perhaps feel threatened by the idea that things might be changing, or feel threatened by someone who is pointing out problems in what they're doing," Dr Natri explains. "No one wants to be told that what they're doing could be wrong, or bad, or unethical, or harmful, let alone that their whole research programme and career has been built upon a foundation that is not good, and that we need to build a completely new framework or paradigm."

I wish I was joking when I say that a prime example of this stubbornness within the autism industry was published in the months spent writing this book. In December 2022, four individuals representing the Autism Science Foundation in New York, the National Council on Severe Autism in California and the University of Pennsylvania shared a commentary arguing for a "full semantic toolbox" in the context of autism research, and that the "censorship" of certain words has a "chilling effect" on the practice.[2]

Words such as "disorder", "deficit", "risk" and "symptoms" are just some of the terms advised against in previous papers, yet defended here by the four individuals. They claim removing words like these impact families for whom autism is "a life-limiting disorder rather than a divergence or identity".

"While terms like 'differences', 'traits' and 'characteristics' may be appropriate to describe some individuals in certain contexts, autism is defined by the American Psychiatric Association in its *Diagnostic and Statistical Manual 5.0* as a 'mental disorder' involving clinically significant impairments in the social communication domain and restricted behaviours," they write. "If autism is a mere 'difference', we risk a future where policymakers are blinded to the dysfunctions and impairments that underlie service needs, while researchers turn away from seeking causes of and treatments for ASD."

The group also go on to claim students and early-stage researchers are "expressing hesitation" about staying in the field due to "regular attacks" on those whose choice of language isn't in line with neurodiversity. They bemoan scientific journals for demanding neutral terms for autism in research papers, and language use being used to argue for lower scores on grant applications, claiming that this leads to the "further exclusion of research focused on profound autism".

"There does not need to be a battle between the two viewpoints around autism vocabulary," they write. "There is room across the spectrum to acknowledge that autism can be a state of being for some, an impairing condition for others and somewhere in between for many."

---

2   Singer et al. (2023).

Except, as has already been explained by Dr Botha and Dr Cage among others, autism is not amorphous or completely removed from the self. Such is the nature of it being a neurological condition that to be autistic is, undisputedly, a state of being, for it affects the way in which we interact with the world around us. These interactions with an overwhelming environment rich with information can be joyous as much as they can be difficult, but in terms of the latter, many autistic people would argue it's the setting or wider society that 'impairs' – or rather, *disables* us, not the condition itself. This is known as the social model of disability.

There's also the fact that the four authors are "all mothers of individuals on the spectrum" – that is, not one of the people behind this argument is sharing a direct, first hand, lived experience of autism in this instance.

Racialized autistics face their own specific barrier in their interactions with academics: the racist trope that they are inherently "aggressive", as content creator and writer Keillan Cruikshank explains. "They understand people of colour – especially Black people – to be aggressive or hostile for even correcting them on something. It's an issue, but because autistic people are that way by nature, and not because we're trying to be rude or anything like that – that's just how we communicate with each other," they say. "Because it's coming from a person of colour, they now have, or they see themselves having, a carte blanche on being more hostile to that person because 'this person is conforming to the stereotypes that I have been taught about Black people or people of colour, so now I have a reason to not listen to them. Now I have a reason to dismiss them and all these other things.'"

Fergus Murray gives another example of this ignorance. "Historically, autistic people have not been taken very seriously by autism researchers. The whole idea that autistic people lack theory of mind has been used as a reason to dismiss autistic people's theories about their own minds," they say. "That's just one of several layers of assumed incompetence around autistic people."

This feels insurmountable as a challenge. The narratives around autism, used to silence autistic people critiquing academics and research on the condition, are shaped by autism researchers themselves. Change is necessary in the industry, yet it seems the current system – as described above – is hampering the move for progress.

Not just that, but the ambiguity around the definition of autism is there to be exploited by autism researchers as they see fit.

"[It] probably allows non-autistic autism researchers to either stay in their silo or stay with the status quo, I think," suggests Professor Pellicano, "rather than challenge the dominant view."

She goes on to add: "The other thing about the working definition which I find problematic is that it is defined on, supposedly, objective behavioural signs and symptoms – you know, observable things. That's what the DSM-5 does, because [autism has] always been judged from the outside and not from within, and so we don't have a really good body of knowledge, even."

Dr Bottema-Beutel also comments on the constraints of the DSM-5. "Many people, for example, who study adulthood will say that 'X percentage of our sample is self-diagnosed because we recognize that there's not equal access to diagnosis', et cetera," she says. "So the gatekeeping of the definition has gotten a little porous, because we don't trust it, because we know that diagnosis exists in a system that is not equitable. It's not objective.

"Even our list of deficits, what really are they based on?" asks Dr Bottema-Beutel. "In my opinion, it's not based on a particularly adequate description of autism. If you look at the DSM criteria, and then you read [Leo] Kanner's 1942 paper, they're not all that different. That was almost 80 years ago, and we have not really filled in the picture to a large extent."

Professor Pellicano continues: "We neither have a body of knowledge, nor do we have researchers and practitioners who really take that body of knowledge seriously, in terms of people's first-person experiences of being autistic," she says. "I'm really interested in how we might introduce a more experiential or phenomenological approach into our understanding of autism and what it's like to be autistic. Essentially, combining those first-person experiences with more kind of third-person, observable, so-called objective behaviours and experiences."

This is the ongoing tug-of-war, almost, between lived experience and objective investigation and analysis. "There is definitely an interest from outside the research community," Professor Pellicano says, referencing the "hundreds" of autobiographies penned by individuals about their own identities, "but within the research community I think subjective experiences have genuinely been eschewed by scientists and researchers. And this goes beyond the field of autism research, I think, because subjective experience is regarded as a problem for science, rather than a resource waiting to be tapped.

"It has meant that autism researchers have tended to privilege the reports from others (especially parents, but also teachers, other informants, as well as lab-based observations) over considering the perspectives of the person themselves," she continues. "This, I think, is despite the fact that there is really, really good work showing that autistic people can, in fact, possess a really deep capacity to reflect on many aspects of the self, regardless of their intellectual or communication preferences."

What doesn't help is that discourse about the condition is still plagued by mentions of "high-functioning" and "low-functioning" autistics. The former often appeared alongside the now-defunct diagnosis of Asperger's syndrome as a classification of autism, whereby the individual does not have an intellectual disability, but both terms have been disregarded by advocates in favour of "high/low support needs". This goes some way to acknowledge that our 'functioning' levels fluctuate based on a variety of factors and environments, rather than being set in stone.

"It becomes a ranking system," Dev Ramsawakh – an autistic, multidisciplinary storyteller from Toronto, Canada – says of the high- and low-functioning models. "I think that categorization, that need to have these clearly defined boxes, is really just a way to keep us from connecting and building our community and having these strong networks of supportive care," they say, "so that we can continue to be marginalized for the benefit of a different group."

Autistic neuroscience researcher Ira Kraemer, known online as 'Autistic Science Person', puts it another way. "It's like, you're either always too 'high-functioning', because you don't know what a real autistic is like, or you're too 'low-functioning' and no one is going to believe you, because 'how would that person have interesting thoughts? There's no way that person made that sentence,'" they tell me. "It's like an unheard community, and then everyone's doing autism research for this community that they never interact with."

When asking autistic advocates and academics what prerequisites they have for connecting with a study, either as a participant or as a collaborator, the value of the research in question is a common theme.

"As a participant in research focused on autistics, I look for a research team that is led by or meaningfully includes an autistic researcher or community member," writes Dr Waisman. "I look at the research question to see if it will serve our community and create better outcomes for us. I check to ensure that the process is respectful of our community and includes intersectional autistic voices in truly meaningful ways. I examine the language used in their invitation to determine if they truly understand our community and how we want to be respected.

"I check their intended outcomes and methods to ensure they are on the right track as far as the science goes, and I look at the reputation of the researcher and the research team to see if they have prior research that is both credible and consequential to our community as defined by us," they conclude.

Of course, the engagement and involvement of autistic people in research (explored more deeply in Chapter 5) has close ties to the wider mantra of the disabled community, which is 'nothing about us, without us' – that anything pertaining to disabled people must, by its very nature, *include* disabled people.

If you wanted to apply this ethos to the specifics of autism research, then it becomes a case of autistic people being involved in studies about their own condition – a commonsense request, but one that can become far more provocative if the question becomes whether autism research should *only* be carried out by autistic people. After all, barriers outlined above and reinforced by allistic academics indicate autistic researchers may be better placed to challenge prejudices, and lead the industry towards improving itself.

It's a question I ask most of my interviewees, and their responses are mixed.

"I wouldn't say that only autistic people should do autism research," argues Dr Aimee Grant, an autistic researcher at Swansea University, "but I think every piece of research that involves autistic people should have a minimum of one autistic autism researcher on the team. It needs to be a researcher who has enough status to be listened to, as too often 'patient and public involvement' representatives are used in a tokenistic way.

"In my opinion, autism research should only be done in a neurodiversity-positive way," she continues, "which means that the researchers *need* an understanding of autism based on up-to-date understandings, including things like the double empathy problem [the theory, coined by UK researcher Damian Milton, that difficulties in empathizing are actually "a breakdown in reciprocity and mutual understanding"[3] experienced by non-autistic and autistic people alike] and monotropism [the concept of the mind being, to borrow from its originator Dinah Murray, an "interest system", whereby autistic or monotropic minds are drawn more strongly to our interests]. Without this, they're just contributing to the existing mountain of evidence based on false beliefs that results in us being misunderstood."

Fergus Murray responds to the question by highlighting another pressing issue. "The key factor is not really whether the researchers themselves are autistic; it's about whether they listen to actually autistic people," they explain. "There are autistic researchers out there who don't listen to other autistic people, who don't see themselves as part of the autistic community, who are quite hostile to other autistic people. That's not necessarily an improvement on non-autistic perceptions. It probably is, a bit, because at least they've got their own perspective, their own experiences to relate things to.

"Much more autism research should be done by autistic researchers," they continue. "No autism research should be done without anyone involved who's autistic. Academia needs to be more accessible to autistic researchers, and it needs to be more friendly to autistic researchers being out, because there are a lot of autistic researchers who are not known as autistic researchers, because they believe it would harm their careers if they became known as such.

"That happens less and less, I think, but I know at least one autistic researcher who I know is autistic, and they know that they're autistic, and the wider world doesn't."

Dr Giwa Onaiwu comments: "I think autistic people should be front and centre, [and] should be given the tools, the

---

3   Milton (2018).

resources and the platform to be able to lead and have meaningful leadership and involvement of these things, but I think that their allies have been important in every single field and every single movement that there ever has been, and I think that this is one where they're needed as well."

It's in the very nature of true allies, of course, to be committed to platforming and engaging marginalized people, because such individuals don't ever centre themselves in the work they are doing in support of another community.

"I think non-autistic researchers can research autistic people or study autism," says Dr Natri, "but it's important to understand the different power dynamics. In any research that is about marginalized communities, whatever that community might be, I think it's really important to make sure that the members of that community are the ones really setting the research agenda and feel empowered in that work, to acknowledge how being in that marginalized position impacts people, what kind of barriers it creates.

"I think there are many non-autistic researchers who have made really valuable contributions to autism research, are true allies and understand the problems and understand the negative bias and our data," she continues. "There are also a lot of people who are not necessarily invested in us or research, but are reasonable people who can be reached, and when you give them this information or context, they understand what the issues are. I think we definitely need allies and non-autistic supporters to make all that work possible."

In autistic academic Dr Dave Caudel's eyes, a good autism researcher is one who has a basic understanding of an autistic person's nature: "the fact that we're detail-oriented to one degree or another, and that we like clear, concise, step-by-step [information]," he explains. "If there's a lot of vague things – there's a lot of vague hand-wavy language – that can induce a lot of stress and anxiety. The more stressed out we are, the more anxious we are, the less likely we are going to participate."

Kraemer outlines more barriers in their response to whether autism research should be limited to autistic researchers. "For me, it's about power," they say, "and the issue is that even, for example, within academia, being an autistic person and getting through graduate school is really hard, getting to be a principal investigator as an autistic person... There's just a lot of barriers. It's not super accessible, and a lot of disabled people say that about academia.

"Even when people want our help and want to ask the community [and] are like, 'how do I do this right?', my answer is really, 'you know what, there's too many barriers for autistic people to even get in'."

Thus, there is a domino effect – or a vicious cycle – at play, where non-autistic academics can warp the understanding of autism, which seeps into the education system, preventing undiagnosed autistics from receiving the support, diagnosis and confidence in their own identity that they need to even enter the research industry and begin to challenge stereotypes and misconceptions.

It's tempting to group all of these arguments and issues under a wider view that a shadowy, mysterious elite is gatekeeping access to research and how autism is described. It's dramatic and conspiratorial, but it's easy to see why when such problems appear to be largely systemic.

Barriers to academia limit the fresh intake of autistic autism researchers into the industry to dismantle ableism and drive change, while in the community at large, advocates are up against tactics which silence and sideline their opinions. If autistic people feel like they aren't being listened to in the research industry or that their judgement isn't trusted – whether as participants or academics – is it any wonder why trust is so low?

There is, undoubtedly, a status quo, and it's the "rigidity of thinking" around it that Dr Caudel cites as a particular barrier for an autistic researcher.

"An autistic person might have a particular approach or idea that they're going to break into the scene and they're going to research their way and such," he explains. "If you're not knowledgeable and understanding of the traditional ways of doing things... What do I mean by knowledgeable and understanding? Not just that you understand how things are done, but why they're done in that way.

"There's usually a good 'why' – it may not necessarily be a 'why' that you agree with – but there's usually a good 'why', and if you come up with your own 'why' that doesn't address those 'whys', then you're not going to be taken seriously. To play devil's advocate, you *shouldn't* be taken seriously," Dr Caudel continues. "I see some early, passionate people who jump into the field and they don't bother to learn the status quo and why that status quo exists. So when they push back with 'I have this radical new idea', and someone's like, 'well here's some of the whys', [and they respond with] 'oh, I haven't thought about that' or 'that's not an issue', it's hard to take you seriously.

"On the flip side, there is that traditionalist fallacy: we do it this way because we've always done it this way," he says.

"The thing that would make the most difference is some sort of union, I suppose," suggests Marianthi Kourti. "One that has to have the difficult conversations and 'these are the terms that you need to hire this person under, this is what the person needs to work for you'.

"I want to have a conversation with a mentor or someone," they add, "[because] things would have been so much different, I would have been so much more prepared. These are not always things you can talk about with your line manager, these are not always things you can talk about with your colleagues. These are not things you can talk about with someone who you feel accountable to. You need another structure in place, because of that pressure.

"So for me, ultimately, what I would want to do is create a sort of centre or union or something that provides people with autistic researchers, with mentors, with someone to talk to if things get hard, with people who help them negotiate the terms of engagement with various projects, within the workplace," concludes Kourti.

I see this as a microcosm for wider society. As if navigating the allistic world around them and all the cultural norms that entails wasn't enough, the atmosphere surrounding autism research appears to come complete with another set of rules and a general groupthink.

Referring back to Dr Caudel's comments around the status quo, how does one balance adhering to the current state of affairs, while also being able to critique it and push for change?

"I find it's much easier to be the 'outside of the box' voice when you first demonstrate that you understand the box," he replies. "First you lay it out and you go, 'hey, this is the part I would like to change, and here are the reasons why I think we should change it'. Researchers, at their core, are people who are obsessed with understanding Mother Nature without their own biases and stuff. I mean, our biases and such always colour things – any decent researcher is at least aware of their own biases.

"If you lay out a logical argument for somebody, where you lay out all the bits that they're going to take exception to, all the nagging questions that they're going to raise, and you give them a satisfactory or at least compelling answer for that, they're going to take you seriously," he adds. "They're going to think about it, and any decent researcher worth their salt is going to change their minds. If you believe in dogma, then it's not science, it's a religion. In my book, you're not a scientist – in fact, you're anathema to science."

Dogma is ideology, and ideology is politics – something which some feel should be stripped away from the factual, objective and impartial practice of science wherever possible.

Yet, when autism research has become as contentious as it has now, that is proving difficult – especially when one considers the fact that when discussing this topic, it isn't long before the name of one controversial individual comes up.

Chapter 4

THE BARON-COHEN LEGACY

Professor Sir Simon Baron-Cohen is the first name that appears when you type "leading autism researcher" into Google, and he is often credited in news reports as such. An academic at the University of Cambridge in the UK, his lengthy career has seen him offer up several theories and papers on autism which have contributed to the existing narrative around the neurological condition, in a way which not every autistic person has appreciated.

In asking to interview him, I am instead offered around five questions which are eventually answered over email by the Autism Research Centre (ARC), the organization of which he is director. With this book already exploring the issue of accountability, the difficulty in asking questions of Baron-Cohen's career and research to him *directly* – work which isn't warmly received by some autistic people – is telling.

I begin by asking if Professor Baron-Cohen feels any pressure as someone considered a leading autism researcher, to which the ARC replies: "There is no particular pressure that comes with our research being in the public eye, as all autism researchers have a duty to be cautious in how they comment on research (e.g. commenting on what conclusions can be drawn from a particular study), to be careful not to use language that could be offensive to or stigmatising for autistic people and their families, and to raise awareness of the needs of autistic people and their families."

Yet in the eyes of some, the work of Professor Baron-Cohen and the ARC is guilty of the very things they say all researchers should avoid. Even as I begin to write this chapter towards the end of 2022, a photo comes up on my Twitter timeline of a book cover from 1999 (now 25 years ago at the time of this book's publication in 2024). It's called *Teaching Children with Autism How to Mind-Read: A Practical Guide*, with Professor Baron-Cohen's name on the front as a co-author.

It's the viewing of autism through a patronizing, "super-human" lens that prompts one user in the replies to reference *Rain Man*, the infamous 1988 film starring Dustin Hoffman as an "autistic savant" which is widely shunned by the autistic community today for its sensationalized depiction of the condition. As psychiatrist Dr Darold Treffert told *The Guardian* in 2018, "only one out of 10 people with autism are savants",[1] and yet the film – in no way helped by the fact that Hoffman himself isn't autistic – established a perception amongst the public that this stat was greater, and that savants (that is, an individual with exceptional, detailed knowledge or talents alongside a developmental condition) were a lot more common across the autistic population.

The 1999 book draws upon the "theory of mind" in relation to autism, something explored by Professor Baron-Cohen. "One such autism-specific [cognitive] deficit is in the child's theory of mind," he wrote in a paper nine years prior, in 1990, "that is, in the ability to attribute mental states to others. This deficit, which shows up reliably across a series of studies, would by itself wreak havoc with the child's social and communicative development, given its critical importance in

---

1   McCarthy (2018).

normal development." The term he would give such a "deficit" is "mind-blindness".

Yet this is not without its critics. In 2011, John Duffy from the University of Notre Dame set out a three-pronged narrative around "mind-blindness", comprising the evolutionary, the imaginary and the tragic.

"A class of people whose evolution may be unnatural, whose minds are so deviant they must be poetically imagined, and who are consequently disoriented as a result of their condition," he explains, "are ultimately understood to be tragic figures." Duffy draws upon language used by Professor Baron-Cohen to describe his theory around autistic people, which is inherently negative: "suffers" and "tragically" being two examples, and we can add "wreak havoc" to that list.

Two years later, in 2013, California researchers Dinishak and Akhtar wrote in an abstract that "mind-blindness" as a metaphor "obscures the fact that both autistic and non-autistic individuals contribute to the social and communicative difficulties between them, carries strong negative connotations, and may impede the recognition that some autistic behaviours are meaningful and adaptive".

In 2019, a particularly damning take came from Morton Ann Gernsbacher of the University of Wisconsin, and Melanie Yergeau of the University of Michigan. They argue that the theory "fails empirically" – in terms of its "specificity, universality, replicability, convergent validity, and predictive validity".

Another contribution from Professor Baron-Cohen is the Autism Spectrum Quotient (AQ), a 50-item self-assessment tool (a shorter AQ-10 exists as well) designed in 2001 to measure "the degree to which an individual of normal intelligence shows autistic traits".[2] Individuals completing the form simply have to confirm whether they slightly/definitely agree or slightly/

---

2   Baron-Cohen et al. (2001).

definitely disagree with the "item" or statement being presented to them.

In focusing on adults who are "high-functioning" or have a
"normal IQ" – IQ, like "high-functioning", having its own controversy around its efficacy as a tool – the study team were effectively excluding autistic individuals with learning disabilities
from those eligible to complete the questionnaire.

Yet as Amsterdam researchers Agelink van Rentergem, Lever
and Geurts noted in 2019, those with a low number of autistic
traits can still answer some of the statements in a way that is
actually more associated with those with a higher number of
traits. They give the example of one statement which states "in a
social group, I can easily keep track of several different people's
conversations", before explaining that an older person may still
give the "higher autistic traits" answer of "disagree" because of
"diminished hearing ability".

Three items later, when the AQ form asks if someone "would
rather go to a library than a party", low-trait individuals could
still give the high-trait response of agreeing with the sentence
because "not just autistic traits but also education could determine whether a person likes libraries".

Then there's the fact that a 2020 study conducted by Taylor
et al., academics from King's College London and the University
of Bath, found the AQ10 version of the questionnaire, recommended by the UK health guidance body the National Institute
for Health and Care Excellence (NICE), has "poor reliability".
They write that their study of almost 6,600 participants "indicates that the AQ10 may not be a psychometrically robust
measure of autism in non-clinical samples from the general
population", and that they would "caution against its use as
a measure of trait autism in the general population" without
carrying out further research on its psychometric properties.

Another issue is best explained in a report by *Spectrum*, in
which they attribute a conclusion to lead author Punit Shah

that "the questionnaire may measure four different traits [of autism], rather than autism as a single, whole construct".[3]

Then there's the matter of Professor Baron-Cohen's "extreme male brain" theory in relation to autism, that expands upon comments made by Asperger. Asperger's comments from 1944, cited by Professor Baron-Cohen in 2002, were that "the autistic personality is an extreme variant of male intelligence. Even within the normal variation, we find typical sex differences in intelligence [...] In the autistic individual, the male pattern is exaggerated to the extreme."

Professor Baron-Cohen reached a similar conclusion in his paper, just with a different wording. "The autistic brain is an extreme of the male brain," he wrote, adding by way of brackets that it is more systematic than empathetic.

The case for "impaired empathising" includes a better score for girls on "theory of mind" tests; females making more eye contact than males; girls developing vocabulary faster than boys; females tending "to be superior to males in terms of chatting and the pragmatics of conversation"; and similarly, that they are better at judging what would be deemed "socially insensitive or potentially hurtful and offensive" compared to males.

Then, on "superior systemising", there's the argument that boys are more interested in collecting items; have a preference for "rule-based, structured, factual information"; and like vehicle and construction-based toys more than girls. Professor Baron-Cohen also claims most autistic individuals are "naturally" drawn to predictable things such as computers, or if not that, then other "closed systems" such as "bird-migration or train spotting".

This seems to me, at least, to be rather stereotypical, piggy-backing off tired notions of what boys and girls are supposed to like. Even some of the statements in the Autistic Spectrum Quotient devised by Professor Baron-Cohen and others, arguably,

---

3   Anthes (2020).

lean more into cliché descriptions of male behaviour, backed up by the wider population studies mentioned by the Cambridge academic.

For example, item six relates to an individual regularly noticing "car number plates or similar strings of information" – cars and vehicles, of course, being stereotyped as being more masculine in nature. "I am fascinated by numbers" can so easily expand outwards to mean mathematics (given how dependent the discipline is on numbers), and then you have Professor Baron-Cohen's argument that this is a highly systemized field and that men score higher on maths tests.

Another instance is item 41, stating "I like to collect information about categories of things" and giving examples such as types of car, bird, train and plant. Again, with reference to Professor Baron-Cohen's comments about males liking vehicles and closed systems such as "bird-migration or train spotting", one has to ask which of these four examples is supposed to concern the "typical" female experience.

The academics behind the AQ stress it is "not diagnostic", but rather a potentially "useful instrument" when it comes to "identifying the extent of autistic traits shown by an adult of normal intelligence". Nevertheless, when combining this with the "extreme male brain" theory of autism, just how much of an impact does the "extreme male brain" theory have on diagnosing autistic women and girls?

Timothy Krahn and Andrew Fenton, both of Dalhousie University in Canada, wrote in 2012 that specific gender expectations in the language surrounding "ASDs" could "perhaps [explain] the under-diagnosis of girls on the autism spectrum".

"If this is correct, seeing ASDs through a gendered lens may be adversely inhibiting early diagnosis and treatment in girls," they conclude, "as well as effectively removing from sight certain 'early interventions' among girls which aid in compensating for developmental differences affecting social skills and behaviour."

They write that Baron-Cohen's extreme male brain theory may – inadvertently – be adding to the kind of systemic issues limiting some autistic girls' and boys' future prospects.

Krahn and Fenton also argue that Professor Baron-Cohen is "misled by an unpersuasive gendering of certain capacities or aptitudes in the human population". They describe the academic's presentation of sex differences as "profoundly misleading" because it doesn't consider other elements that affect how both boys and girls are socialized.

"There is simply no substantive reason for thinking that males are *biologically constituted* to excel in areas that require aptitudes in abstract reasoning (i.e. systemizing acumen) or that females are *biologically constituted* to excel in areas that require aptitudes in intuitive reasoning or emotional intelligence," they add, stating that in doing so, the "extreme male brain" theory of autism both "plays upon" and "reifies sex stereotypes" by treating autism as an "inherently masculine" condition.

One particular study in 2017 from a trio of University College London academics – Rachel Loomes, Laura Hull and William Polmear Locke Mandy – explored the gender bias in autism diagnoses in significant detail, with one suggested, potential reason for this being "key professionals (teachers, family doctors, paediatricians, psychiatrists, psychologists, etc.) holding gender stereotypes that ASD is a male disorder, reducing their sensitivity to autistic symptoms when they occur in females".

No specific mention of Professor Baron-Cohen here, of course, but it sure reads as an indirect reference, at least, to the academic who first popularized the notion that "the autistic brain is an extreme of the male brain" (note that the ARC reject the claim that the "extreme male brain" theory suggests only males are autistic).

In 2019, a "theoretical review" of the "extreme male brain" theory by Cambridge academic Rosalind Ridley was published, with Ridley writing in the paper's abstract that Professor

Baron-Cohen's hypothesis is "comparable to the claim that, because on average men are taller than women, extremely tall women have 'extreme male height'", and that such a "stereotypical view of gender fails to recognise the overlapping diversity of cognitive styles found in males and females".

In fairness, it would be wrong to solely pin the blame for the under-diagnosis of autistic women and girls on Professor Baron-Cohen's "extreme male brain" theory, but it's one of his many contributions to the field of autism research that has attracted controversy, and the gender stereotypes certainly don't help alongside the misdiagnoses and misunderstanding autistic females can and do experience. A report by the UK's National Autistic Society (NAS) in 2012 notes females are more likely to be misdiagnosed with another condition (42%) than males (30%).[4]

Of course, in addition to these criticisms, the binary comparison between male and female completely neglects non-binary people. This is explored further in Chapter 6.

When I ask if Professor Baron-Cohen acknowledges that the "extreme male brain" hypothesis has caused harm in relation to the under-diagnosis of autistic women and those assigned female at birth (AFAB), the ARC replied "there is no evidence as far as we are aware" that such a theory has led to under-diagnosis in respect to these two demographics.

There is no concession, at least, that the theory may have – either directly or indirectly – contributed to the wider pool of issues autistic women and AFAB individuals face when pursuing a diagnosis. Instead, the ARC says: "In the period of 1978–1994 (approximately) the sex ratio of those receiving an autism diagnosis was 4:1 (male to female). The prevalence of autism in that period moved from 4 in 10,000 to 1 in 500 in that same period. With the inclusion of Asperger's Syndrome into the autism

---

4   National Autistic Society (2012).

spectrum in 1994 and the steady rise in prevalence of autism to 1 in 100 in 2009 (from a study by our group) and now 1 in 44, the sex ratio has shifted to about 3:1 or even 2:1 (male to female) in most studies."

The ARC spokesperson continues: "The extreme male brain theory was published in 2002 and yet the rate of diagnosis of autism in females began to increase from before its publication and has continued right up to the present time."

They go on to reference the Cambridge Lifespan Asperger Syndrome Service (CLASS), later rebranded to the Cambridge Lifespan *Autism Spectrum* Service, as the first UK clinic to "accelerate the late diagnosis" of autism and what was then known as Asperger's syndrome. "The clinic was inundated with women seeking a diagnosis and we became more aware of masking and camouflaging as women told us in the clinic how they are 'pretending to be normal'," the ARC explains, adding that they would not use that terminology themselves, and that it was instead the name of a book from 1999.

"Over the subsequent 20 years the clinic has diagnosed hundreds of women as autistic and continues to do so," they continue, before addressing the issue of masking in particular. "Masking or camouflaging comes at the expense of mental health, as it means many girls and women feel they have to hide their autism and 'cannot be themselves'. Often poor mental health such as anxiety and depression leads to diagnostic overshadowing, such that an autism diagnosis is missed.

"In all likelihood, camouflaging is a reflection of stigma that has surrounded autism, particularly in those assigned female at birth. Thankfully today autism is less stigmatised, which is terrific, though there is still much work to be done."

There's also what they call "misunderstandings" around the "extreme male brain" theory, the main two being that it argues "autistic people lack empathy" and that "autistic people are hyper-male in general" – both of which the ARC stresses are not true and not asserted by the theory itself. The ARC references a 2018 study conducted by researchers from its own centre (Professor Baron-Cohen is listed as one of four authors, with David Greenberg as the lead)[5] as a "big data" paper which supports "the science behind the theory". One finding was that in both datasets analysed – one involving more than 670,000 people and the other including some 14,300 individuals – autistic individuals on average were "masculinised" regardless of their reported sex.

This is mentioned in an article for *The Conversation*, penned by Professor Baron-Cohen and the other three co-authors behind the 2018b study, and published in the same year.[6] The two aforementioned "misunderstandings" are addressed in turn, starting with the issue of empathy.

"The evidence suggests that it is only [...] 'theory of mind' that autistic people on average struggle with," they write. "As a result, autistic people are not uncaring or cruel but are simply confused by other people. They may miss the cues in someone's facial expression or vocal intonation about how that person is feeling. Or they may have trouble putting themselves in someone else's shoes, to imagine their thoughts."

The group stress autistic people do not lack empathy, because they are concerned when someone is experiencing pain or suffering and want to offer support.

They then turn to the misinterpretation, prompted by the "extreme male brain" theory, that autistic people are "hyper-male" – which they say is "not the case".

The academics write that although autistic people tend, on average, to score closer to a male profile of results on tests concerning empathy and systemization, they are not typically "hyper-male" – not least when it comes to other classic

---

5   Greenberg et al. (2018b).
6   Greenberg et al. (2018a).

variations in the sexes such as aggression, as autistic people have been found to be gentle characters rather than overly hostile.

A reminder of Professor Baron-Cohen's conclusion back in 2002: "The autistic brain is an extreme of the male brain." This was based upon a selection of supposed common behaviours in men, backed by studies of the broader population, which made the case for stronger systemization over weaker empathy. The selective approach that leads Professor Baron-Cohen and others to cite areas where autistic people *do not* match male characteristics – such as the argument that "they are not extremely aggressive, but tend to be gentle individuals" – is the same tactic he uses to argue for the "extreme male brain".

To put it another way: you cannot pick and choose male characteristics to back up the "extreme male brain" hypothesis and dismiss criticisms. Arguing the autistic brain is "an extreme of the male brain", without a wide-ranging, holistic view of the male brain and all its behaviours, reveals a flaw in the hypothesis. It inadvertently concedes that the theory has limitations.

Another concession comes from Professor Baron-Cohen in November 2020, when he tweeted that he "[retracts] the EMB [extreme male brain] terminology and [calls] it the Empathising-Systemising (E-S) theory". The ARC made a similar admission in their response to my questions, stating "it may be beneficial to change its name, perhaps to the hyper-systemizing theory".

It certainly could have avoided reinforcing harmful gender stereotypes and biases by focusing on empathizing and systemizing away from the lens of gender – even in the name alone. Nevertheless, the alleged damage caused by the theory has been done.

On the theory of mind hypothesis, the ARC said it was based on "experimental evidence" from 1985, "long before autism was commonly diagnosed in people without learning disabilities".

"Despite this, the theory has been widely supported by

hundreds of studies, although it has required different tests for those without learning disabilities. An example is the 'Reading the Mind in the Eyes' Test, in which autistic people consistently score lower compared to neurotypical people," they write, citing Professor Baron-Cohen's 2015 paper on the test.

The ARC went on to add: "To be clear, we do not think that autistic people lack empathy. There is no suggestion in the theory of mind hypothesis that autistic people have reduced agency."

I also ask the centre why trust in autism research is so low, to which they reply: "Historically, autistic people with and without learning disabilities have been subjected to unethical and sometimes horrific treatment, including electric shocks as punishment, compulsory sterilisation and even murder, for example during the Holocaust.

"Even now, many autistic people experience abuse and exclusion across multiple areas of life, including at the hands of those who are supposed to protect them.

"In research, the traditional model can be seen as being done 'to' people rather than 'with' them," they continue, "because it has not often included autistic people in meaningful ways. Some are concerned that biological or genetic research may lead to a prenatal test as part of preventing autism in the future and can see that this has happened in the case of Down's syndrome.

"We understand that factors like these can make it difficult for some people to trust researchers when they say they aim to improve quality of life, rather than to prevent autism. We have stated many times that we are opposed to prenatal testing for autism, but some people find that difficult or impossible to believe."

The ARC does, however, acknowledge that there are "many different, and sometimes conflicting, views among the autism community".

"We hear from many autistic people and their families who tell us they are highly supportive of our work, including our biological and genetic research," they explain. "Nonetheless, we are committed to building trust where it is lacking. We are increasing our community engagement, so that we hear and understand all points of view and can take them into account as early as possible when designing future projects. This starts with transparency about the work we are doing and clear explanations of our aims, methods, and the potential impact on the lives of autistic people, including the timescale for this impact.

"Where there is a perceived risk of outcomes such as a prenatal test, we have a responsibility to clearly explain our understanding of that risk, as well as the predicted benefits.

"Another important factor is for all researchers to provide concrete information about the use of participants' data, especially when this involves DNA," the ARC continues. "Many want to know that their data will not be shared with researchers or organizations who may want to develop a prenatal test for autism, or who may want to cure or prevent autism. Again, for clarity, at the Autism Research Centre we do not want to do any of these things."

In their response to the question over whether the medical/biological model and social model approaches to research can coexist, given their contrasting ideology, the ARC says they "don't see any necessary tension" between the two as "both can be useful".

"Autism has been shown to involve biological differences and we also accept that many difficulties faced by autistic people can be understood to be a result of obstacles in society," they explain. "However, we are moving away from thinking about autism as a medical condition.

"For example, we are now thinking and talking in terms of autistic 'people' rather than 'patients', and referring to 'features' rather than 'symptoms' of autism. There is an ongoing challenge for researchers, who must publish their work in journals that still require traditional terminology that the researchers would not use elsewhere, such as the official diagnostic label 'Autism Spectrum Disorder'.

"At the Autism Research Centre, we are actively talking to journals so that we can influence them to think about autism in a less medicalised way, as many members of the autism community have told us they would prefer," they reveal. "We initiated this about 20 years ago, so that articles from our group used the acronym ASC (Autism Spectrum Condition) rather than ASD (Autism Spectrum Disorder) and we were willing to argue with journal editors who tried to insist on the latter.

"We are pleased that over that 20-year period, the term ASC became widely adopted, especially in Europe, although nowadays we simply use the term 'autism' to cover people across the whole autism spectrum, as it is shorter and avoids the potentially medical overtones of 'condition'."

In the case of those medical studies in which they are working with medical or biological data, the ARC has committed to working with the autism community to establish a "data-sharing committee" for any future research projects, as well as one current and ongoing study exploring the DNA of autistic people.

"Such committees must include autistic people and their decision-making rules must be transparent," the ARC says. "This will show the autism community that requests for data sharing will be vetted in a way that takes into account their concerns and preferences, and safeguards against the research being used for harm.

"We know that there will not be a consensus within the autism community and some people will continue to oppose certain types of research or even specific researchers," they go on to add. "As in any large group, there are many perspectives, and it is not realistic to expect to reach one agreed point of view. Nonetheless, we are committed to ongoing work over the long term, to build trust and ensure that our research leads to positive outcomes for autistic people.

"Researchers have a responsibility to talk to funders about the most appropriate stage for community engagement in all projects, and to ensure that adequate time and resources are allocated for this work, so that it can be done early enough and thoroughly enough to impact on the design, and even the focus, of new studies," they conclude.

This is outlined further in response to one question I ask about how Professor Baron-Cohen centres and uplifts autistic people and the community's views as a non-autistic or 'allistic' researcher.

The ARC replies: "For every research project, we are committed to conducting appropriate levels of engagement with the autism community to ensure the views of autistic people and their families are taken into account. This aspect of our work is growing, and we are developing improved ways to engage with the autism community from the earliest stages of research design.

"We have created a new Communications and Community Engagement team to support our researchers to reflect on and develop their community engagement practices," they go on to add. "This team includes both autistic and non-autistic people, as does our wider research team, and we expect that more autistic staff and students will join us over time."

It's clear from the above that the ARC has taken steps to improve its approach to community engagement in recent years – not least since 2021, when one project launched by the centre would become infamous for its lack of significant consultation...

Chapter 5

THE ART OF CONSULTATION

M aking himself comfortable on the red BBC Breakfast sofa, Professor Baron-Cohen explains some of the hallmark traits of the condition to which he has dedicated his academic career.

"It is a disability," the autism researcher says in the interview from August 2021. "It affects social skills, communication [and] being able to manage unpredictable change. Some of these kids or autistic adults get very stressed at change, but they just think differently. Their brain is developing differently right from the beginning. They're processing information differently.

"It's a complex condition," Professor Baron-Cohen continues, "and this new study is trying to understand why some autistic people have no language, and others have good language; why do some have learning difficulties, and others don't, [and] why do some people have good mental health and others don't."[1]

The study in question is Spectrum 10K, led by Professor Baron-Cohen and the University of Cambridge, in partnership with the Wellcome Sanger Institute and the University of California Los Angeles (UCLA). The 10K refers to their target: to

---

1   BBC Breakfast (2021).

obtain the DNA of 10,000 autistic people to "look for the genetic causes of autism and the environmental ones".[2]

In submissions to ethics boards, it was stated there were "no direct benefits to participating" in the study.[3] The very group Professor Baron-Cohen was trying to recruit also had concerns, too.

On 4 September that year, a group of "autistic community members, academics, representatives of advocacy organisations, and allies", organizing under the name Boycott Spectrum 10K, issued a statement criticizing the project.[4] It covered seven areas of concern: transparency; biodata regulations; issues around consent; the "suitability" of researchers involved in the study; conflicts of interest; ethical issues; and how said ethical issues interact with concerns around transparency. "In short," they wrote, "it is, at best, a study lacking not only autistic co-production, but also lacking a thorough understanding of autistic experience and wellbeing. At worst, this is a thinly veiled attempt to DNA data mine at the expense of the autistic community."

On data collection, there was an inference from the group that the study – in requiring every participant to agree to have their "anonymised data and DNA" used, potentially, in "future studies, shared with academic collaborators and included on external databases for future use" – could breach GDPR.[5] The European Union (EU) legislation, adopted before the UK officially left the bloc in January 2020, states that the "controller" of an individual's personal data must "be able to demonstrate that processing" of said data is in accordance with the regulations – as one would expect it to.[6]

Yet Boycott Spectrum 10K argued there were grounds for

---

2   BBC Breakfast (2021).
3   University of Cambridge (2020).
4   Boycott Spectrum 10K (2021).
5   Boycott Spectrum 10K (2021).
6   Legislation.gov.uk (2016).

fearing "data use violations" based on the data the Cambridge study was requesting, and how it would be used. They claimed: "Consent for S10K is sought for DNA collection, data collection, and complete access to medical records without clear description as to what the project aims to do; how any of this data will be used by the project; who that data will be passed on to in the future; or how it will be used in the future."

Part of the problem is the fact autistic people aren't entirely against medical research into the condition, as previous chapters have noted. "We fundamentally recognise the need for good, robust genetic and biological research in order to aid greater understanding of the impact of conditions that have genetic roots and can have life-limiting effects or impact on the wellbeing of autistic people," said Boycott Spectrum 10K. "However, we have grave issues over how the data from genetic research could be used, and the very obvious lack of safeguards for its future use."

The Spectrum 10K team have responded to concerns around the legality of its data collection by stressing the data will be pseudonymized and stored on secure, password-protected servers at the University of Cambridge in compliance with GDPR and the Data Protection Act.

They add data will also be stored securely in databases when shared for other research purposes, using full anonymization.

"Approximately, as things currently stand – and there is scope for discussion about this – the data can be analysed for about 25 years once the study starts, essentially," the researchers said in a webinar in May 2023. "That would mean other researchers can also analyse the data and analyse it for approximately 25 years. In [these] 25 years, people are free to withdraw at any point, and their data can be deleted from future analysis."

The academics then said once further analysis within the 25-year period is complete, the data is archived (at which point is becomes de-identified), which means it can no longer be analysed.

As for data protection, the team outlined two routes to keeping this secure. The first relates to a setup where the data can be downloaded onto "university-approved servers" but not to personal computers, and usage is bound by "strong data transfer agreements". The second, meanwhile, concerns researchers having access to a central database in which they can select the variables they wish to investigate, and it is "close to impossible to download any data locally".

It is a "very closed system", the researchers said, whereby the Spectrum 10K academics have greater control over the sensitive data, such as limiting external access to a specific time period.

Boycott Spectrum 10K's September 2021 statement also cited an academic who outlined the misguided contrast between where autism researchers *think* the community is with genetic studies, and where it *actually* is: "My sense is that genetics research projects like Spectrum 10K are requiring autistic people to have a level of trust in autism research that most autism researchers absolutely have not earned."

There was a marked difference between what was on Spectrum 10K's website (tying biology with wellbeing) and a grant application to the Wellcome Trust. The latter, approved in 2018, requested funds for a Common Variant Genetics of Autism and Autistic Traits (GWAS) Consortium, in which one of its aims is to "recruit 10K autistic individuals from the UK and where possible, their families" to conduct "genome-wide genotyping".[7] This, of course, would become Spectrum 10K.

The application also said the project would "allow us to better understand the biology of autism, improve on existing methods for diagnosing autism and investigate if there are genetically-defined subgroups of people with autism". This

---

7   University of Cambridge (n.d.).

raised eyebrows within the autistic community. While it was included in descriptions on Spectrum 10K's website, wellbeing – as noted by Boycott Spectrum 10K – wasn't mentioned once in the summary offered to the Wellcome Trust.

The full grant application had been obtained from the University of Cambridge through an FOI request by Panda Mery, an autistic researcher. It stated Spectrum 10K wanted to "identify modifiable risk factors for autism".

A separate section of the document, outlining the "impact, novelty and expected outcomes" of the study, revealed researchers would "investigate the biological correlates of autism" – that is, "which tissues, gene-sets, cell types, and developmental periods are enriched for common genetic risk for autism".

"We will further investigate heritability across subtypes, sex-specific effects, and effects of social and non-social domains of autism," they added.

The Spectrum 10K study team acknowledged "wellbeing" was missing from the Wellcome Trust grant summary in a letter to the HRA in January 2021, in which they said it was a "very early summary" of the project, produced when the study was without a name.

"Some aspects of the study evolved further after this was written," they write, "for example following consultation with our Advisory Panel [...] we included additional 'wellbeing' measures, including those relating to quality of life, self-medication, and strengths of autistic people."

They also said they added measures in light of the coronavirus pandemic, which revealed autistic people were "found to have poorer outcomes", and that their aim of investigating genetic subgroups for autism "is consistent with improving wellbeing".

The application had international support. Among the 11 organizations listed as backers were France's Institut Pasteur; Denmark's Aarhus University; the Queensland Institute of

Medical Research in Australia; Vrije Universiteit in Amsterdam; and Massachusetts General Hospital in Boston. The aforementioned SPARK study was also one of them.

Then there's the matter of "subgrouping", which Boycott Spectrum 10K claimed could "potentially be used to separate autistic people into groups which are deemed 'low-functioning' [...] or valueless to society, or 'high-functioning' [...] and therefore have value to society". Referencing the decision to bring a diagnosis of Asperger's syndrome under the "more accurate" single diagnosis of autism spectrum disorder (ASD) – a decision made in the DSM-5 – the campaign group said a return to subtyping as laid out in the Wellcome application would, "for many autistic people and their families, be a very unwelcome step backwards".

Concerns over subgrouping weren't helped by the discovery of a job advert from 2019 for a research assistant for the then unnamed Spectrum 10K, which said the study "aims to understand the broad heterogeneity within autism that ranges from learning difficulties through to talent".[8]

The implication was there that autistic people with learning disabilities cannot be talented. The study team would later clarify that "people who are autistic and who have learning disabilities can be talented" and that they "absolutely" see all subgroups as equal.[9]

Not only that, but Professor Matthew Hurles, co-principal investigator for Spectrum 10K and director of the Wellcome Sanger Institute, is leader of the Prenatal Assessment of Genomes and Exomes (PAGES) study – a project which, in his own words, investigates "the genetic causes of developmental anomalies that are identified during prenatal ultrasound screening, with the aim of improving the prognostic

8   British Neuroscience Association (2019).
9   Hopkins Van Mil (2023d).

information that can be provided to parents".[10] It's one area that has ignited fears Spectrum 10K could lead to the development of prenatal screenings "used to identify autistic babies in utero and give parents the opportunity to abort them".[11] Spectrum 10K researchers insist the study "does not aim to develop a test for autism".[12]

Meanwhile at UCLA, Dr Daniel Geschwind, another co-principal investigator, was revealed to have been affiliated with the now-defunct organization known as Cure Autism Now. When approached by me for *indy100*, a sister site to *The Independent*, he said in a statement: "Cure Autism Now (CAN) was founded by parents of children with autism in the late 90s to fund research and bring attention to autism. CAN was acquired by Autism Speaks and has not existed for over 10 years."[13]

An explanation from Spectrum 10K, offered up to the Health Research Authority (HRA) watchdog, shed further light on the issue. Dr Geschwind had been asked to chair the brand-new Scientific Advisory Board of CAN, and he also developed the Autism Genetic Research Exchange – a dataset containing data from "more than 1,700 families with over 3,300 autistic individuals", and one that Spectrum 10K hope to analyse, subject to the necessary approvals.

Spectrum 10K continued: "The title 'Cure Autism Now' was meant to bring attention to the condition, start dialogue and discuss what it would actually mean to make progress and develop treatments in this condition. The work of [CAN] to help those with the most severe disabilities emerged at a time when very little was known about the condition, very few worked on it and there was certainly not a recognition of those autistic

---

10   Wellcome Sanger Institute (n.d.).
11   Boycott Spectrum 10K (2021).
12   Spectrum 10K (n.d.).
13   O'Dell (2021a).

people who value autism as part of their identity, which is a newer phenomenon."[14]

Other problematic organizations emerged under Spectrum 10K's "autism advice" webpage on their website. The page – later removed following my report in March 2022 – included Child Autism UK (who were "instrumental in establishing ABA in the UK") and Autism Independent UK, also known as The Society for the Autistically Handicapped (TSAH).

A spokesperson for the latter organization – Keith Lovett – would go on to tell me that "handicapped" and "mental retardation" (which is mentioned on its 'What is Autism?' webpage) are still appropriate terms to use, in the context of disability and autism "in a medical setting".

The latter of the two is commonly referred to as "the r-word". According to the Special Olympics, the term is "a form of hate speech", and those who use the word "often do so with little regard for the pain it causes people with intellectual disabilities and the exclusion it perpetuates in our society".[15] "Handicapped", meanwhile, is considered an outdated and offensive term to describe disability.

Another section of TSAH's website republishes a report on "sexuality and autism" from the Treatment and Education of Autistic and Related Communication Handicapped Children (TEACCH) – a document which Lovett said was "written by others" and "given" to TSAH. It reads: "we think it is helpful to allow these individuals to have contact with the opposite sex. Even severely autistic individuals seem to know the difference between men and women and to be more attracted to members of the opposite sex.

"Providing heterosexual experiences such as classroom programmes, leisure activities, and residential living situations

---

14 Baron-Cohen (2021).
15 Special Olympics (2023).

seem to, in some way, meet the sexual needs of these clients. The more of these opportunities we can provide, the more appropriate their sexual behaviour will be."[16]

Lovett said the statement was "not necessarily correct", and when asked about Autism Independent UK's stance on LGBTQ+ people who may experience same-sex attraction, his initial response was "n/a".

A follow-up question led to him adding: "I say this as it is dependent on the severity of autism and other cohabiting conditions. For example, most may understand or be attracted to the opposite sex, some may see you as a moving object that does certain tasks.

"I feel the higher up the continuum you go the higher the attraction is likely."

In a statement issued before the details on the "autism advice" webpage were removed, a Spectrum 10K spokesperson said: "Under our 'useful links' section, we listed the largest autism-related charities in the UK. Entry in this list does not represent an endorsement by Spectrum 10K but we acknowledge that this may not have been clear and have decided to remove the page from our website.

"We do not endorse Applied Behaviour Analysis, as we recognise concerns about the approach. We would like to see more research conducted to explore alternative approaches."

They continued: "As above, we have decided to remove this page from our website. According to Google, Autism Independent UK used to be called The Society of the Autistically Handicapped.

"Clearly, this language is out of date. We do not use the term 'handicapped'."[17]

Then there was the matter of how and when autistic people

---

16   Autism Independent UK (2021).
17   O'Dell (2022a).

themselves were consulted about the project. Spectrum 10K listed several autistic individuals as ambassadors on its website, which made clear that "an advisory panel of autistic people and their families" were consulted during the study's design phase.

"They approached me last year [2020] wanting me to promo it," autistic speaker, consultant and trainer Connor Ward wrote on Twitter at the time. "I wanted a conversation to voice my concerns. We had that conversation. They never followed up and today I see they ignored my advisories. They knew a year ago yet chose to ignore."[18]

Numerous problems have been unearthed as part of my reporting on Spectrum 10K, but the apparent lack of truly meaningful consultation with autistic people underpins a significant number of them. It's arguable that other concerns around the research having undertones of eugenics, and hesitancy around data security, could have been remedied by involving more autistic people in the process ahead of it being given the green light. It's this important element of autism research which this chapter will focus on, while telling the story of the controversial project. What constitutes meaningful consultation, and indeed, what does it have to offer?

In the case of Spectrum 10K, a concession on their lack of community engagement came in September 2021, a month after its launch. "From the feedback we have received from autistic people, their families, and charities," Professor Baron-Cohen wrote in a statement, "we can see that we need much wider consultation, that we were not clear enough about the aims of the study, and that aspects of our study need further discussion".[19]

The study was paused, with the promise of a "meaningful consultation" with autistic people and their families to be carried out before it would relaunch. A month later, in October, it was

18 Ward (2021).
19 Spectrum 10K (2021).

revealed researchers had brought on board stakeholder engagement firm Hopkins Van Mil (HVM) to facilitate such a conversation. This would come in three phases: 15–20 autistic people, along with some parents and carers, would first decide who would co-design the consultation; the group would co-design it in the second phase before being launched in the third and final phase.

However, on 2 September 2021 – the same month in which they would announce the pause and upcoming consultation – a member of the ARC made their feelings known on the ongoing public scrutiny to an individual from the Royal Wolverhampton NHS Trust – one of the NHS sites that had agreed to recruit participants for the study. The Trust had written in an email earlier that day that they had received "some negative feedback on our Trust social media page about the Spectrum 10K study". The example they gave was one which said the "autism community are against it".[20]

They weren't the only ones to pass on negative feedback. Another NHS trust notified Spectrum 10K of concerns raised with them from "a number" of their experts by experience. The clinical research team leader at Sussex Partnership NHS Foundation Trust (SPFT) told the academics: "I had enquired about whether there were concerns raised that could be addressed by your study team, however they have said that the feedback is categorical. As such, we are sadly going to have to take the decision not to proceed with the study at SPFT."[21]

In their response to Royal Wolverhampton, the ARC made clear they were aware of the situation. "We are preparing a response," they said. "In the meantime, we have posted a statement on Twitter and an automatic reply to the study email account. We recommend at present that you do not engage with trolls targeting Spectrum 10K on Twitter."

---

20 O'Dell (2022b).
21 O'Dell (2022c).

The remarks shocked autistic people online once published. It is not known who made this comment, but still, to some in the autistic community, it felt as if the researchers were branding members of the very same group they wanted to recruit as "trolls".

I was issued a statement from a Spectrum 10K spokesperson: "We recognise that the vast majority of critical comments about Spectrum 10K are made by people who are voicing legitimate concerns," they told me over email. "This is why we are co-designing a consultation process in order to listen to as many of those concerns as possible.

"However, several members of the Spectrum 10K team have received online abuse. An email was written after somebody who was not part of the core team reported 'being trolled' after receiving abuse on Twitter, and regrettably their language was echoed in this email," they added.

Yet it wasn't the only email from the study team to use this language. An email sent a month before the one to Royal Wolverhampton, this time to Pennine Care NHS Foundation Trust, used exactly the same pejorative term – and indeed statement – to respond to concerns which the NHS site had passed on to researchers.[22]

This time, no statement explaining a second use of the word "troll" was provided.

They would later clarify further, saying "we certainly do not see concerns about autism, or concerns about the autism community, as trolls", but in April 2022, Spectrum 10K decided they would no longer respond to my journalistic enquiries.

"Since October 2021, we have responded to all of your journalist requests," they wrote. "We are a small team and this takes a lot of time.

"One outcome from Phase 1 of our consultation was the importance of keeping the momentum going on Phases 2 and 3.

---

22 O'Dell (2022d).

Therefore, we have now decided that we need to prioritise consulting with the wider autism community.

"With regret, we cannot continue to respond to any further requests."[23]

This decision from researchers was taken against an autistic journalist who was often being praised for keeping the community informed about what the study was saying privately.

In that same month, I had published news of a draft Frequently Asked Questions (FAQ) document from the study team, in which they ask themselves the question: "Are there autistic people involved in the process? How will you identify what is and is not eugenics? These teams have been known to lie in the past."

One of the many downsides of their decision to refuse to respond to my press enquiries is that when I asked them whether this was an admission of dishonesty, or a note on the tone of autistic people critical of the study – either option is damning – they declined to comment.

I would have to wait until May 2023 for an answer, when I asked the research team the question again during a Zoom webinar. Their response was that the comment was one from social media they copied and pasted into the document "so that we remind ourselves that this is a point that we need to address". They added they are "not in the business of lying" but rather "in the business of transparency and honesty".[24]

Whatever the context, the remark is indicative of the hostile relationship some autism researchers have with the autistic community.

Maria Scharnke pointed out a flaw with the feedback Spectrum 10K chooses to accept during our conversation. "Of course, anybody who gives them genuine feedback about ethics

---

23 O'Dell (2022e).
24 Hopkins Van Mil (2023a).

concerns must be 'high-functioning' for some reason," she says, "[so] how can they possibly, ethically suggest that these people [who are] 'low-functioning' – that they are claiming do not have the intellectual capacity to have any ethical qualms – how are they then suggesting it's ethically OK to take their DNA?"

In another message from the advisory panel, obtained under FOI, a health professional from Cambridge Community Services NHS Trust emails the study team: "Do you have the Terms of Reference for the advisory group please? I need to check its [sic] not a conflict of interest to be the local PI for one of the recruiting organisations and be on the advisory panel."[25]

It's understood this particular individual became a member of the panel before the NHS Trust was set up as a research site for Spectrum 10K.

In response, a study representative attached the Terms of Reference and revealed "there is nothing about conflicts of interest" in the document. The health professional eventually decided to step down from the panel.[26]

At the same time as that process was under way, the HRA were investigating the study in response to complaints from members of the public. "We have written to the study team with the concerns raised with us and have asked them to reply. This doesn't mean that they have done anything wrong, but is the way that we manage complaints in line with our process," they said in a statement issued in September 2021.[27]

Correspondence sent a month later, which I also managed to secure under FOI, shed light on those concerns – and some related to engagement. "Allegations that ambassadors [of the study] have used racist and transphobic language" was one,

---

25 O'Dell (2022e).

26 O'Dell (2022e).

27 Health Research Agency (2021, 2022).

and another was that "the study team have not responded to concerns that have been raised with [them] about ambassadors being insulting and dismissive of concerns which have been highlighted to them".[28]

Ambassadors were proving to be somewhat of a headache in terms of publicity. In their first consultation update since October 2021, Spectrum 10K wrote in May 2022 that they were scrapping the ambassador role altogether. It would be impossible, they said, for academics to keep the representatives "up to date as the consultation progresses" because elements of the project can "change very quickly".

"This risks placing ambassadors in a situation where they are asked questions that they cannot answer," they added, "simply because we have not had time to bring them up to date. We want to avoid any risk of public confusion about the project, and focus entirely on the consultation."

May also saw the HRA conclude its investigation into the Spectrum 10K study, stating that its favourable opinion of the project "still stands", but "some of the issues raised" through the organization's complaints process "could have been considered" during the initial ethics review.[29]

These covered nine areas:

1. the conduct of ambassadors;
2. the affiliations of the research team;
3. allegations the team have ignored autistic people's concerns and not centred their views;
4. support has not been provided for autistic individuals triggered by the study;
5. information in the patient information sheets and consent forms lacks clarity, including on the use of data;

28 O'Dell (2021b).
29 Health Research Agency (2021, 2022).

6. a "discrepancy" between the project's stated aims and its methodology, and it's unclear why DNA data is needed to achieve said aims;

7. the collection and storage of a "huge body" of genetic data from a marginalized group is unethical, and there's a lack of safeguarding over the data;

8. young people and carers cannot make an informed decision over their genetic information, and when they reach the age of consent, the withdrawal policy does not allow for a participant's data to be completely removed;

9. previous data removal requests have not been actioned.

A tenth consolidated requests from a research ethics committee.

Spectrum 10K's responses to the concerns contained in the HRA's final decision were substantial. The ambassador accused of racist and transphobic remarks assured the study team it wasn't their intention, which aligns with a message I obtained in June 2022, written by the Spectrum 10K researchers and sent to the HRA, in which the academics wrote: "We can see that some people interpreted certain posts as racist or transphobic.

"However, in discussion with the relevant ambassador, we were reassured that this was not the intention. None of the social media posts reviewed were found to contain unambiguously racist or transphobic language."[30]

Meanwhile, the project's "sponsor" (it has two: Cambridge and Peterborough NHS Foundation Trust and the University of Cambridge) said none of its members have published opinions or carried out research which contradicts Spectrum 10K's stated aims.

"The sponsor has informed us that neither the Autism

---

30 O'Dell (2022g).

Research Centre (ARC) nor Professor Baron-Cohen have links to ABA," the HRA's decision reads, "with Professor Baron-Cohen having written against 'radical behaviourism' (of which he would see ABA as one example) as far back as 2014."[31]

On the matter of Dr Geschwind's affiliation with Cure Autism Now (CAN), it was explained he chaired the group's scientific advisory board in the 1990s (including when the organization was later taken over by Autism Speaks), but never received money from them for this or for his research. They also made clear that "language, concepts and priorities of the autism community have changed over time and the aims stated by CAN nearly 20 years ago are not in line with the aims and values of Spectrum 10K, which Dr Geschwind shares". The ARC and Professor Baron-Cohen are involved in the AIMS-2 trials backed by Autism Speaks, the controversial US charity which also funded a 2012 predoctoral fellowship into "hypersensitivity in autism".

The report also noted that the "sponsor" has stated that the "Spectrum 10K team and the ARC are ethically opposed to any form of eugenics, believing that autism is an integral part of human neurodiversity".

Spectrum 10K researchers apologized "unreservedly" for any distress caused to members of the autism community and said they linked to organizations offering support on their website. They also believe collection of genetic data from autistic people is not unethical if the purpose is to "increase understanding about which genes influence particular outcomes", and added that they will design a data-sharing policy with the autism community.

The study team added that "discussing the concerns raised by some people in the autism community and ensuring that they

31   Health Research Agency (2022).

signpost people to appropriate support where it is needed will be fundamental during the consultation".

They also said all withdrawal requests had been actioned with formal confirmation sent to all individuals concerned. Those who requested "no further use" of their data following withdrawal have had any submitted samples destroyed, they said.

Similarly, on the consent of children and young people, the study sponsor said Spectrum 10K includes child assent (that is, an agreement given by a child under the legal age of *informed consent*, which is 18) in the sign-up process, and participants will be asked to consent to continued involvement when they turn 16 during the study.

Then, on documentation, Spectrum 10K said the consultation will offer a "further opportunity" to ensure participant materials are "clear and transparent". Referring to the Wellcome Trust application summary not mentioning wellbeing, the research team clarified the published aims of the study are "focused on understanding wellbeing".

"Where wellbeing is mentioned throughout their website and documentation, it is in relation to understanding how biology and experiences shape wellbeing.

"They see this type of research as forming an important early step in providing evidence that can be used to improve wellbeing in the future, with the direct improvement of wellbeing being outside of the scope of the current research grant," the HRA's findings read.

Nothing in this section addressed the concerns over the grant application saying it will investigate "which tissues, gene-sets, cell types and developmental periods are enriched" for a "genetic risk" of autism, however.

The study team revealed that more than 4,300 participants had registered and consented prior to the study's pause, but it was clear the Spectrum 10K researchers were still having problems with engagement. Alleged remarks from ambassadors online may well have pushed potential participants away.

There was, however, one proposal from Spectrum 10K researchers – floated in their grant application to the Wellcome Trust – which looked to encourage participation in their study. A £10,000 prize draw would have given 100 registered individuals £100 each, if this ethically questionable proposal wasn't abandoned by the research team.

They "wanted people to sign up because they were interested in the research, rather than for financial reasons", the academics said.[32]

It was feared some of the factors influencing recruitment would influence engagement with Spectrum 10K's consultation when launched. The study team were apprehensive that there were "a few people who want to volunteer" not to help improve the study, but to hinder the consultation process, warning in an email from September 2021 that there was a "high risk" of this happening.

Phase 1 of said consultation saw HVM speak to 23 autistic people and six non-autistic parents or carers, clinicians or representatives from charitable organizations. Those involved in the consultation co-design in the second phase, the agency reported, would have to agree that they "will not prevent the process moving forward to the consultation phase".[33]

Spectrum 10K put it another way in their summary: "Those involved should agree to participate to improve the study, not stop it."[34]

This stipulation was a tricky one to strike, however, as HVM also made clear that "those who have been critical of the study should be involved in this process". One Phase 1 participant

---

32 O'Dell (2021c).

33 O'Dell (2023).

34 Spectrum 10K (2022).

even told the consultants: "Critics are so important in order to ensure the highest standards are met. Criticism pushes research forward, improves processes and outcomes."[35]

Another individual is quoted as saying "reciprocity" is key to the consultation process. "So if people are giving you their time, energy, emotions and they're getting nothing in return," they explain, "it's not a co-design relationship. It's more like opinion harvesting. So make it an ongoing [sic] and mean it."[36]

Those involved in considering who should be involved in the co-design of the consultation discussed four principles which would make the Phase 2 co-design meaningful: it would need to be inclusive "from the very beginning to the very end of the dialogue process"; make time to establish relationships whereby people "know they are valued" and trusted; be respectful of all participants' views; and be iterative and have ideas and solutions "continually proposed, tested and evaluated by the group".

In November 2022, news of Phase 2 was released. They previously said this was expected to take place in July of that year, but it concluded three months later, on 31 October.

At this stage, conversations about Spectrum 10K took the form of discussions and workshop activities in a dedicated online space, one-to-one interviews and meetings. It involved 95 autistic people (including those with learning disabilities and some who are, themselves, parents of autistic children), 16 non-autistic parents or carers, and the Spectrum 10K team.

A report on the findings from this stage was published on 19 December and revealed that 429 applicants had applied to be a part of Phase 2, of which 130 were selected as co-designers, before 19 people withdrew from the process because they couldn't find the time to take part.

Twenty-two to 24 people were involved in four Zoom

---

35 O'Dell (2023).
36 Hopkins Van Mil (2022a).

workshops (the same individuals each time), before these participants and 79 others were invited to take part in activities, polls and discussions in their own time, held on an online space.

Eight co-designers had one-on-one interviews with a facilitator from HVM – either on Zoom or over email. Only seven people were against genetic research into autism to some extent (either "completely" or "against, but not completely"), compared to 65 who were either quite or wholly supportive.

Thirty-nine people were in the middle, as being "undecided on their view" or responded with "don't know".

By the end of Phase 2, there were seven agreed points upon which the final consultation could be considered successful, which reflected the four pillars set out in Phase 1:

- participants acting with "openness and transparency"
- the information provided being "accurate, accessible and clear"
- the consultation providing "a balance of positive, negative and neutral aspects of autism"
- it "has influence on the study"
- it "shares learning"
- it establishes a "constructive space" which allows for the opinions of those consulted to be heard
- it builds trust in both the study and the research team.

Another section of the report details four principles for the remainder of the consultation:

- to "build trust in the process"
- to "make real and positive change to the Spectrum 10K study"
- to demonstrate the consultation "involves and has been designed by" autistic people
- to create a space which allows for "constructive

discussion" and for people to respond to "a range of views".

Trust in the process, the report would go on to add, links to concerns that advocates who have "called for a boycott of Spectrum 10K will refuse to take part in the consultation".

"This would be disappointing for Phase 2 co-designers, who want to ensure that all views on Spectrum 10K are considered, including those who have been critical of the study," it reads.

Similarly, on transparency, it states: "Trust cannot be built if people perceive there to be any hidden information or agendas within the consultation. Co-designers want to know that this consultation is a genuine attempt to improve the study. They believe that showing that this consultation is different to those who appear to be making an insincere attempt to gain people's views is important."

This is why the report states that transparency, in relation to Spectrum 10K, concerns information about who is involved in the research, who is funding it, how such funding could influence study outcomes, and what the actual aims and objectives of the study are.

Meanwhile, the survey making up the third and final phase of the consultation would now be released in "mid-January 2023" (not September or October 2022, as initially intended), with the results analysed at the end of the month.

The consultation responses would form topics to discuss with respondents through workshops and online forums between February and March 2023, before analysis and reporting on "what was said and how to improve/change the study" would be published in "late March". A working group to co-produce the recommended changes would then get to work from April onwards.

The consultation survey was actually launched in March

2023, before closing at the end of May. More than 500 people submitted a response, of which 409 were autistic people.[37]

Alongside the survey, five webinars encouraged attendees to put their questions to the research team directly. These sessions – held across the month of May – covered topics such as the aims of the study, data security and the inclusion of autistic people without capacity to consent. Those who attended the online Zoom sessions were asked not to live-tweet or screenshot the "confidential" sessions, with HVM instead promising to publish transcripts of the webinars on their website in the "coming weeks" after the last webinar took place.[38] Such a decision meant answers from the study team to questions asked would not be readily available to survey respondents who couldn't make the online sessions, but nonetheless wanted to provide a more informed response to the consultation based on the responses given.

In fact, months would pass without a single transcript being released. All five were published by HVM in September, and saw the Spectrum 10K team deny a "discrepancy" between a description of the study provided to one NHS trust and public messaging around the project; acknowledge that the word "risk" in relation to "genetic risk" was "inappropriate"; make the case for post-natal testing instead of pre-natal testing (as it "removes any risk that the test would be used for prevention"); and that data obtained for Spectrum 10K could be analysed for "up to 25 years".

At this point, it must be noted that the ARC was given the opportunity to comment on the issues raised in early drafts of both this chapter and the previous chapter.

They appreciated it, but rather than issue specific comments or responses to the findings contained in the two chapters, the

---

37   Spectrum 10K (2023a).
38   Spectrum 10K (2023b).

ARC instead issued a brief statement. "In these chapters, the author has gathered together the information he has collected about Spectrum 10K and research conducted by Professor Baron-Cohen," it reads. "On reading these chapters, we realised that the author's interpretations are often so far from ours that we would need to comment throughout. Rather than do this, we encourage the reader to remember that there are often alternative interpretations and conclusions that can be drawn and that some information may be incomplete and/or inaccurate."

Spectrum 10K continues to spark animosity from both sides: the autistic community and researchers. The environment for creating a meaningful consultation – one which could see Spectrum 10K moulded to better suit the needs of autistic people, and thus encourage more registrations – is strained and complex. Even when academia is, according to Boycott Spectrum 10K, "starting to accept that the most valid form of research" pertains to co-production, it's clear the industry still has some way to go to make such an approach the norm.

How can conditions be created for positive and truly *meaningful* consultation, and what would that even look like?

"It means involving autistic people from the start and at every step along the way," says Fergus Murray. "There's an infuriating tendency in the autism research community of deciding what they're going to do, and then asking autistic people about it later.

"Autism charities do much the same thing as well, and obviously, there are a few problems with that," they continue. "Once they've decided what they're going to do, it's a bit late to ask people if that was the right thing to do at all. If they've got a vague idea for a project, and then they go and talk to some autistic people, that's different."

Connor Ward adds: "When you feel you've got true engagement [...] the person feels comfortable enough that they aren't masking or they're masking to a degree where they feel able to deliver their true authentic opinions. Obviously, they may want to mask in whatever way in the actual interaction aspect of it, but the opinions and thoughts that they're giving shouldn't be altered by that – that would be good – and that it's actually listened to."

The Academic Autism Spectrum Partnership in Research and Education (AASPIRE), based in Portland, Oregon, established its own guidelines to "promote the successful inclusion" of autistic adult participants in 2019. Launched in 2006, the partnership emerged from the observation that "despite great increases in the amount" of autism research, there's been "little focus on how to improve the lives of adults on the autism spectrum", with autistic adults "not usually included as resources or partners in autism research".[39]

The guidelines emphasize the importance of accessible consent procedures and qualitative interview guides, "multiple modes of participation" to increase the inclusion of autistic participants with different needs, and avoiding the risk of "undue influence and exploitation" while at the same time "maximizing autonomy and inclusion".

It's under separate guidelines for successful co-production with autistic autism researchers that the word "trust" is mentioned, where it stresses studies should "regularly focus on building and maintaining trust" – something I would argue applies on a participatory level, too.[40]

Further criteria on how this can be achieved are particularly insightful, underscoring the clarification and solidification of shared goals, and celebration of success. These guidelines also state studies should "actively listen to community partners' views and demonstrate that you value the expertise that

---

39 Academic Autism Spectrum Partnership in Research and Education (2020).

40 Nicolaidis et al. (2019).

comes from lived experience"; "follow through and implement the group's decisions and regularly report back on progress"; and "regularly evaluate and improve the collaboration".

Collaboration, of course, which occurs at the very beginning of the process. This is as much a case of inclusion as it is for practicality. Academics, already under pressure during the research process, can be saved from a lot of administrative issues by working with autistic people from the outset, rather than rushing to consult only when problems are identified – as what was seemingly the case with Spectrum 10K. "Nothing about us, without us" could not be more apt when it comes to autism research.

Those involved in Spectrum 10K's consultation process appeared to be alert to the nuances around autistic involvement in research, and community engagement. In August 2022, autistic autism researcher Leneh Buckle was announced by HVM as the co-lead for the consultation. Her hope, she explained in a short blog post, was that her history of working for the autistic community and carrying out community-driven research will help autistic people "trust that my intention is to listen to them" and ensure "their voices are heard".

As such, it was hardly surprising that Buckle had concerns over tokenism and being "just another tick in a box". She adds that she was willing to "fight for a legitimate role if necessary", but it hasn't been necessary so far, with her opinion being "highly valued" and the research team receiving training from her in effectively working with autistic people as opposed to the "generic training" from neurotypical-led organizations.

Then comes a caveat from Buckle. This doesn't mean she can guarantee the consultation results "will be taken on board" by Spectrum 10K researchers, but she can say that the consultation in itself is "genuinely co-produced".

When such collaboration occurs, there will of course be compromises on both sides. The challenge is establishing a conclusion upon which both parties are satisfied. "Autistic people need to be assured that the researchers are doing it for the right reasons, based on a modern understanding of autistic people," says Ward, "to which unfortunately, a high percentage of clinicians and researchers don't have a modern understanding, and therefore that trust isn't there and won't be there for a long time."

Such a "modern" approach, he later goes on to explain, would concern the social model of disability, a move away from the deficit-based view of autism and an acknowledgement of neurodiversity.

Liz Pellicano, whose work focuses on community involvement, says it's all about power. "Sometimes, speaking to researchers, I don't think they quite understand that they need to relinquish that in order to do participatory research," she argues.

Yet as much as this is about early, meaningful consultation, there is also an integral issue around who is invited to shape and participate in research – and perhaps more importantly, who *isn't*.

Chapter 6

THE INVISIBLE

"Intersectionality has been neglected in autism research and practice," write Dr Monqiue Botha and Dr Kristen Gillespie-Lynch in a 2022 paper for *Human Development*. "Intersectionality teaches us that we must understand differences *within* the autistic community if we wish to help all autistic people experience the dignity they deserve."

A 2022 North Carolina study by Boyd et al. into the representation of race and ethnicity in autism research in the field, in which more than 1,000 articles on autism intervention research between 1990 and 2017 were analysed, illustrated clearly the lack of understanding around this very issue. Only a quarter shared data on these two demographics.

Of these studies, the paper concluded, Hispanic and Latino participants made up just 9.4%, Black autistics were next at 7.7%, while Asian participants only made up 6.4% of the total.

What barriers might be at play which lead to racialized individuals being underrepresented? "One theory has been that we express our traits differently," notes Dev Ramsawakh. "Whether it's because of cultural differences, whether it's because of how people read us and the way that we express our traits.

"For example, not being able to have control of your tone – your volume and tone – that is not weird in my culture," they add. "So, for West Indians or Caribbean folk, we're loud. My whole childhood, when I was with family, we're loud, we're expressive. We have very enthusiastic tones, you know exactly what we're feeling when we're feeling it, and so for me, that was a very typical way to act."

Another issue is at play, too. "There is a lot of white supremacy in research and in science in general," he says. "I mean, if you look at the history of science as we know now – this Western model of science – there's a very dark history with white supremacy.

"You've got phrenology [the pseudoscientific study of a skull's shape to suggest mental abilities], you've got eugenics, you've got all of that," Ramsawakh continues. "So, a lot of the time, I feel like it's a continuation of those ideas [...] and then we decide who gets access to different resources based on diagnoses, then you can help one group sort of succeed and achieve and move forward, while the rest of us sort of don't."

The issue is systemic. "I have this very unique experience where I get to see exactly how every system built by colonization essentially works together to create these barriers, and that they aren't just isolated from each other," they explain. "They aren't just individual systems [...] If you take them apart and you look at them individually, you can say, 'Oh, this is inclusive, this is equal, this is whatever', but when you put them together, you can see how one system allows another system to enact harm, or neglect folks, or to promote white supremacy.

"When you have multiple people who have multiple identities, you're going to get a completely different view of what autism in the autism community is like," he says. "This very mainstream view of autism is from a very particular group, and doesn't really align with the experiences that other folks have."

Ramsawakh isn't the only one to mention white supremacy's influence in autism research. When I ask Keillan Cruikshank about the barriers preventing racialized folk from participating in research and becoming researchers, he replies: "They both stem from the same sort of issue of racism, white supremacy and anti-Blackness being part and parcel to how psychology and psychiatry function in terms of being participants.

"Most researchers, they study people from rich, educated, Westernized, industrialized backgrounds," they continue. "They mostly pick white participants because most of the researchers are white. They only look for how it looks to white people, people who they can relate to on a human level.

"In terms of getting into research, the fields, of psychology and psychiatry are still hostile to people of colour who try to get into the industry, because it's hard to get into positions where you can have your research be listened to and be given the grant funds and stuff to do the kind of research that you want to," adds Cruikshank. "A lot of white people are psychologists, they don't recognize when Black autistic people or children are in distress, and they don't pay attention to when their Black caregivers are talking about the signs that they should be looking for."

He concludes: "It takes longer for Black people to recognize that they're autistic and we have to deal with more distress in life, because the people who are in charge are the gatekeepers of the access to care and stuff like that, they don't understand our pain."

I ask Cruikshank how one can even begin to dismantle something as embedded in research as white supremacy. "I think part of it has to come from within the community itself," they reply, "because there's a hesitancy within the community to talk openly and honestly about the role that it all plays in who gets to be seen as autistic and who doesn't and the representation that we have in the media. There's this huge hesitancy – especially from white autistic people who have a large platform – there's like a hesitancy from them to talk about it. It makes it harder for autistic people of colour to speak up about it, because they don't want to have to endure all the racism and all that stuff from those people's followers and fans.

"I've had it happen to me where I speak out about like, 'oh, hey, this person isn't including this perspective', or they're not talking about how being white is [seen as] an essential part of the autistic experience," he continues. "There's a lack of sharing and engaging in the material that people are talking about because they would rather protect the white person's feelings, in order to have that access to power, as opposed to sticking up and protecting the people most marginalized in the community."

When there is such an oversight in the industry and community around the experiences of racialized autistic people, there can certainly be a sense of pressure felt amongst Black autism researchers looking to enact change. "I think what's difficult is that feeling of knowing that the moves that you make may have, or will have, an impact on the next Black female to come into this lab, or the next Black female for other researchers to come across, or for a participant to come across," Clíona Kelly, a doctoral student at Aston University in Birmingham, England, tells *Spectrum* in 2020.[1] "I've got this need to be not just good, but I need to exceed that, in order for people to appreciate what I'm doing and who I am and why I'm here.

"I think it's only recently that I've kind of been like, 'OK, this is getting heavy. This shouldn't be a load that one person needs to take on.'"

In her comments to the same outlet, University of Texas PhD student Desi Jones says: "We need to increase the representation of Black autism researchers across all career levels, and we need more people in tenured positions who can serve as mentors for new students, so that we can have this community aspect again.

---

1   Coombs (2020).

"It's not enough though just to increase the representation of Black researchers; you have to support us once you hire us."

Dr Morénike Giwa Onaiwu agrees. "It can't stop there, because I think you can flood a room full of stuff," she explains. "So I think increasing the representation, but also I think we really need to stop and do things a lot differently.

There are, they say, so many barriers facing Black autistic people. "In terms of being autistic, period, regardless of race; being Black, regardless of neurology; and then with the two overlapping it's even more so," she tells me. "Being Black, or even being a person of colour at all, or anyone really who has multiple marginalizations, you aren't a whole person to research. Even if they mean well, are well intended, you're basically a sum of your deficits. You're these disparities, you're all these things that are wrong."

She continues: "You only exist as an outlier, and you exist by people who are interpreting your experiences or your outcomes by their standards, or by what they understand or see, not with an understanding of who you are, or what you know, or what the context is.

"So in terms of the research itself, when you're looking at the pool of participants, and you see how minimal representation there is of people like you, when you look at the research team, when you look at everyone that's making decisions or is in charge, there's no one that's like you. No one has a name like yours, no one understands what's really happening."

The extent of the involvement, Dr Giwa Onaiwu adds, is surface level with so much inference. "No one knows how to just be direct," she says. "It's all about implications and beating around the bush and not getting to the point. There is so much ableism and there's such a sense of entitlement [...] Even the terminology that is used is really stigmatizing and not at all life-affirming for a person that's disabled or neurodivergent. Then, when you combine the two, it's almost like you have to be one or the other.

They give an example. "'This is the way people with *this* disability behave, so this should be how you behave or speak or think', even if that doesn't take into account the cultural aspects of who you are, or the way that you present," she says. "So it's like, you can be a self-advocate, or the parent, but you can't be the researcher. You don't know anything, you're boxed in. It's very frustrating. There's a lot of 'invisibilization', a lot of erasure.

"It's sad to me that if I'm wanting to look up research about people who look like me and my children, and share our neurology, I'm not going to find anything that's neutral or strength-based. Everything I'm going to find is going to be negative – that's the only thing that people care to capture about us."

This is the reason why Dr Giwa Onaiwu went to graduate school. "I was tired of being treated like that person, that mom, that ignorant person. So I felt like, 'these people don't respect me, they're never gonna respect my gender or my race or my neurology, but they respect pieces of paper'," they explain. "They respect titles. So if I can at least say, 'OK, you can't pull the wool over my eyes because I do understand, I have this equivalent level of knowledge', then at least they are forced – not because they want to, but they have no choice – to give me truthful answers and not fudge things or obfuscate or whatever, but I've learned that's not necessarily the case."

According to the writer and researcher, there's not been a lot of growth when it comes to autism research, with few studies looking into areas relevant or important to the autistic community.

"I think that's going to continue to be a problem and we can have all of the wonderful, really beautifully created websites and brochures and programmes with all of these buzzwords about inclusivity," they continue, "but until we actually make our practices inclusive, until we make the applications such to where they are cognitively accessible to people, to where we have mentors, and we have people – not just the janitor and not just the person who answers the phones – to look and sound like our community, then it's going to continue to be this way."

Conversations with other multiply marginalized autistics also appear to point towards a monolithic and restrictive "autism" which lacks and disregards diversity and its nuance. Bodhrán Mullan explains: "I think depending on the researcher, you can have the thing where you try and say, 'I'm autistic', and they go, 'but you're gay'.

"There's also the thing where they go, 'autistic people, they don't want relationships, they don't want to have sex' kind of thing," they continue. "There's a kind of desexualization and I think a lot of queerness is hypersexualized, so you have that barrier of trying to convince [them]. But if you try and convince them, you're considered one or the other, not both. They sort of downplay that queerness if you're autistic, saying, 'you don't really know what you're doing, do you?'"

Except, Mullan adds, autistic people do know their own minds. "Because autistic people are required to do deep dives into their own psyche and personality from a young age, because of the fact that we don't fit the norms," he says. "If you're not diagnosed, then you don't know why you don't fit the norms – you think you're a monster – so you have to do the deep dive to know who you are. I just considered the idea that gender is a social construct – we don't vibe with those, that's kind of why we have a condition."

In Marianthi Kourti's opinion, autism has been designed to fail since the beginning. "If we look at it from a sociological lens," they explain, "what you see is that, basically, the people who are diagnosed are white boys who don't live up to their potential. So you have white middle-class boys who have no reason to not do well, and yet, they don't do well, and people are wondering, 'Why? How could someone who has every privilege in life still present in a way that doesn't reflect that and [end up] with an autism diagnosis?' – which isn't to say that autism isn't biological, which isn't to say that autism isn't a part of who you are as a person.

"What it *is* to say is that a lot of people who didn't have those privileges growing up – and that would include people of colour, people growing up in very poor families, be it women and girls, trans people – they have also had these reasons that diagnoses of autism were missed," concludes Kourti, adding that such an approach is also "hyper-capitalistic".

Ira Kraemer knows this oversight all too well. "As a non-binary person, autism research currently is still very binary," they tell me. "I've seen very few studies that include other gender identities, and I think that's a huge barrier, and also just people who don't really understand how to create options for gender identity respectfully in a survey. I also consulted for someone on that, and you don't just put 'transgender' – 'woman, man, transgender'.

"So there's just sort of logistical things that some cis people don't understand in terms of language and understanding gender identity," they continue, "but then aside from that, it's hard to be respected for your pronouns as a non-binary person, and I think any trans person can relate to that."

Kraemer goes on to cite the "extreme male brain" and "female protective effect" theories as two examples of a gendered approach to autism. The former, as a reminder, was first proposed by Simon Baron-Cohen in 2002 and suggests autism "can be considered as an extreme of the normal male profile". It adds that, on average, autistic people will "show a shift towards 'masculinised' scores on measures of empathy and systemising". It was later renamed the "empathizing-systemizing theory" by Baron-Cohen, who retracted the original "extreme male brain" phrasing.

Meanwhile, the latter theory simply suggests females are protected biologically from developing autism – a hypothesis which tries to explain in some way why around four times as many cisgender men are diagnosed as autistic in comparison to cisgender women.

"There's so much like binary gender stuff when it comes to autism research that it's like non-binary people don't exist," Kraemer explains. "I'll see interesting studies about autism and I go, 'Oh, that's great, so I know how men and women feel, so how do non-binary people feel about that?' It's just sort of an afterthought, and it's ironic because there are a ton of LGBTQ+ autistic people, and especially trans autistic people, who exist in the community, so they're leaving out a giant cluster of people.

"You're kind of like invisible within a community that's already invisible, and it's a little disheartening."

This idea is explored further by Noor Pervez, community engagement manager at ASAN, who expands upon the issue of diagnostic disparity. "For autistic trans people, for autistic people of colour, we're likely to get diagnosed later in life and we are likely to just, broadly speaking, be entering community discourse and community spaces at a point such that we tend to have more conversations with people in similar identity groups," he explains. "What I mean by that is basically that – similar to what you'll see in the LGBT community, where folks kind of develop their own patterns around language and reclaiming slurs and certain standards of behaviour with different generations – the same tends to be true of autistic people.

"Certain things are assumed when you have the knowledge of yourself for longer," Pervez continues, "versus people who might be newer to the community who might be learning terminology for the first time or who might not have had exposure to, say, broader self-advocacy history or might still be learning. They are going to have different input sets of data coming in, for lack of a better word."

This culminates in what Pervez argues is a "decent chunk" of the community – not least older autistic people – struggling to navigate where they fit in such a space. "[It has] this odd dual-ended effect where for some people, that can kind of push them to want to participate in research, to be kind of like, 'Oh, well, I guess I represent something that's really unusual, I guess I should make sure that that's there,'" he says. "But then there's also people who might blame themselves and feel like, 'Well, maybe I'm just really not in tune with what's best for the community, maybe I don't know. Maybe I guessed wrong, maybe I'm not even autistic, I don't know. People are treating me like I'm very much not part of the community, so maybe I'm not. Maybe something is wrong.'"

Ableism is indisputably a barrier facing autistic women and non-binary people, but as Lydia X Z Brown – a senior advisor at the Autistic Women and Non-Binary Network – explains, there's extra issues affecting this demographic too. "We face the additional compounded and amplified impacts of misogyny, and patriarchal values in shaping both societal expectations of who can and should be a producer of knowledge, and consequentially, who can and should be in positions of influence and decision-making capacity within academia, including research," they tell me. "So the prototypical image in Global North, white Western societies in particular is that a researcher and academic scholar – a person who should be in a position of authority – should be white, should be wealth privileged, of upper class, and should be non-disabled.

"So, anybody who does not conform to those expectations and their actual experiences, their characteristics, or their identities," Brown continues, "is already at a severe and substantial disadvantage that is reinforced both through those cultural values and societal expectations, as well as through the structural barriers that arise out of those values and expectations."

Ramsawakh comments: "I think a lot of it is because as soon as you identify yourself as queer – whether it's gender or sexuality – a lot of authority figures start to dismiss you and

dismiss your traits and things like that as deviant or just at-
tention-seeking. Especially in current times, where one of the
major pushbacks against queer culture is, 'oh, people are just
saying they're queer to be cool', or 'it's trendy' or it's whatever.

"I know a lot of folks who specifically don't pursue official
diagnoses because of the way that they'll be treated if doctors or
any authority figures think they're autistic," reveals Ramsawakh.
"I've recently even been seeing a lot of discussion around con-
servatorship, incompetence, and medical decisions, and just
agency in general. Your agency can just be taken away from you
with that autism diagnosis. It's very strange that neurotypicals
will be like, 'Oh, it's a trend because people want to be quirky'
and all of that, when it's like, 'well, it's actually very dangerous
for us to acknowledge these things', especially because there
are a lot of people who want to take advantage of autistic folks."

Fergus Murray agrees: "There are biases in academia towards
conventionality, which hits queer folk in much the same ways
that they hit autistic folk. There's obviously a big intersection
there in terms of being perceived as a bit weird, and people
holding that against us."

Prejudice isn't helped by not having the lived experience,
either. "As most researchers haven't got any experience being
semi-speaking, they make bad assumptions," explains Jamie
Knight – an autistic writer, podcaster and digital accessibility specialist – and his plushie, Lion. "For example, assuming
I'll always have someone with me doing support if I am using
AAC [augmentative and alternative communication]. Another
common assumption is to assume that ability and speech are
linked – for me they are not."

Jamie and Lion tell me they move between semi-speaking
and non-speaking, dependent on the environment, energy and
the situation at hand, as well as other factors. "I can sit in the
cafe writing code used daily by millions of people having not
mouthed a word," they add.

The other barrier to non-speaking autistics is patience. "I need time to communicate," Jamie and Lion explain. "I've often taken part in research and the researcher has been in a rush and that's created more pressure and made communication harder."

Similar problems present themselves when it comes to non-speaking autistics looking to become academics. "[There's] a lack of respect for our expertise and value," they add. "Another issue is grouping. Researchers tend to be from a single area – sociology, neurology, [speech and language therapy] et cetera – and some of us don't fit neatly into that system."

Digital accessibility barrier can be at play, too. "When we can't use the tools due to the barriers in the tools, it's often seen as a lack of skill, rather than an exclusionary tool," the pair tell me.

There do, however, seem to be some small steps being made in the industry. Dr Heini Natri feels like there are "lots of autistic female researchers", but isn't sure of the sex ratio. "I think just in general, for multiply vulnerable or multiply marginalized people, when you're facing kind of that negative bias in many different ways, it obviously has consequences," she comments. "If autistic people have to work three times as hard, then an autistic trans or autistic Black person is going to have to work like ten times as hard to even be taken seriously or be allowed in those spaces."

The best way of addressing the underrepresentation of certain demographics of autistic people is, naturally, to increase that representation. Though simply stating this without interrogating the deeper symptoms that contribute to this phenomenon would be ignorant, condemning autism researchers and all those with an interest in the industry to repeat the same conversations.

It's clear that the problem of viewing autism as a singularity, rather than with all its wonderful, intersecting complexities, is present here, too. It affects the consideration of multiply marginalized autistics in research, and tragically, it contributes to a cycle in which the same white, male, middle-class, cisgender view of autism prevails. It limits the range of experiences we hear from in autism studies, and shapes the narratives that dominate media portrayals and news articles about us.

Just as much as autism researchers need to embrace a diversity of opinion in the industry, they too must accept the diversity of autistic people – and charities have a significant part to play in that.

Chapter 7

THE TRANSLATORS

It was, they now say, a "mistake", yet many of the very community Autism Speaks seeks to represent view their controversial 2009 advert "I Am Autism" with contempt and disgust.[1] Its infamy remains more than a decade later, and its messaging continues to stain an organization that now so often has the "S" in "Speaks" replaced with a dollar sign by autistic people – a nod to where countless autistic people believe their priorities lie. The charity, however, says 86¢ for every $1 donated "goes directly to research, advocacy, programs and services", it meets standards for charity accountability set by the Better Business Bureau each year, and that more than 1.6 million autistic people and their families have been helped through their "free services and supports".

"I am autism," a grumbling male voice says, over short video clips of children and young adults. "I'm visible in your children, but if I can help it, I am invisible to you until it's too late [...] with every voice I take away, I acquire another language."

It goes on. In painting autism as this invisible, airborne threat which "hovers around" people, the commercial also claims autism will ensure marriages fail, families are bankrupted, and

---

1   Autism Speaks (2016).

parents are robbed of "your children and your dreams". All of this will happen, the narrator says, while parents "have no cure".

It was only in 2016 that Autism Speaks removed the word "cure" from its mission statement,[2] now opting instead for "creating an inclusive world for all individuals with autism throughout their lifespan" and ensuring access to "reliable information and services". They add that they do this through "advocacy, services, supports, research and innovation, and advances in care for autistic individuals and their families".[3]

As for what they fund, multiple annual reports in recent years give the biggest slice of the pie chart to the vaguely titled "understanding and acceptance", defined in their 2018 report as "awareness efforts in support of people with autism". The 2021 annual report for 2020–2021 lists just 21% of funding ($15 million) to "services and support", compared to half ($36.8 million) on "understanding and acceptance".

The non-profit has also been shunned over its use of a blue puzzle piece logo – often described as a "hate symbol" for implying something is "missing" – and its MSSNG genetics project to identify "many subtypes of autism".

Though in a section of their website titled "Questions and Answers", Autism Speaks outlines the changes the charity has undergone since it was set up in 2005, namely that it has "learned more about autism and the lived experience of autistic people".

The webpage goes on to state that Autism Speaks aims to build a society where "total acceptance" is standard.

If we are to examine autism research in forensic detail, as this book very much hopes to do, then the role of charitable organizations – like Autism Speaks – in funding and supporting academia must be scrutinized.

Dr Amanda Roestorf is the head of research at the charity

---

2   Fox (2016).
3   Autism Speaks (n.d.).

Autistica, which is more focused on the autistic person's experience. "It's crucial to have data to advise and influence key partners to implement proven solutions that change autistic people's lives," says Dr Roestorf. "We know that research has the potential to transform the everyday lives of autistic people by making sure that treatments, support and services are based on the latest evidence.

"We use research to get the answers that are needed for public policy decisions," she adds. "With research, we and other charities can help every autistic person to live a happy, healthy, long life."

Back in 2015, Autistica began looking into the research priorities of autistic people, publishing its top 10 areas in a report a year later:

1. Which interventions improve or reduce mental health problems experienced by autistic people?
2. Which interventions effectively develop communication and language skills in relation to autism?
3. What are the most effective ways to provide adult social care for autistic people?
4. Which interventions lower autistic people's anxiety levels?
5. What are the appropriate environments and supports to help autistic people achieve the best outcomes in areas such as education and social skills?
6. What support can be given to parents and other family members to help them better care for and understand their autistic relatives?
7. How can the diagnostic criteria for autism become more applicable to adults, ensuring individuals are diagnosed appropriately?
8. How can employers be encouraged to introduce person-centred interventions to support autistic people in the workplace?

9. How can people better understand sensory processing in relation to autism?
10. What improvements and adaptations should be made to services for autistic people to ensure their needs are met?

The Autistic Self Advocacy Network, a US-based non-profit run "by and for" autistic people, also has several areas which they think require more research:[4]

- What are the different causes of meltdowns and sensory pain for autistic people?
- What can help autistic people to control their bodies, and what's responsible for autistic individuals having issues with this?
- Why are some autistic people affected by mental health conditions such as anxiety, and what can help them?
- Why are many autistic people also epileptic, and why do they have connective tissue disorders or have trouble sleeping? What will support them with these conditions?
- What can be done to help increase the inclusion of autistic people in society, including in the workplace?
- What support needs to be offered in order for autistic people to live their best lives?

They add that genetic research may "help to answer a couple of these questions", but most listed above "aren't about genes at all".

Meanwhile, the NAS said they had carried out a study into what they called "life challenges" for autistic people.

"A lot of times, charities will ask, 'what do you think the most

---

4   Autistic Self Advocacy Network (n.d.).

important thing is for us to campaign on or do something about are?'" explains Tim Nicholls, head of influencing and research at the charity. "So we asked a slightly different question because actually, [with] 'what's the biggest issue you face?', you don't get the answer coloured by what people think you should be working on, but what's really important for them.

"The thing that came up as a priority then was mental health, but the other priorities included getting a diagnosis, education, care and support, and employment. So that's essentially how we know what the main priorities are."

These findings – namely that mental health was of particular importance – would go on to prompt further questions. "What we need to unpack from that is, how much is that poor mental health a consequence of other things failing, and how much is it a discrete mental health problem?" continues Nicholls. "So we know that people are on long diagnosis waiting times, children aren't getting the right support in school, people aren't getting any help at home through social care. We know that that stress and anxiety is going to build up and could contribute to anxiety and depression.

"If you remove those things from it," he proposes, "what will be the remaining mental health aspects of that?"

Equally, there's red lines on what type of research charities collaborate on, and the more ideological issues behind it. "We don't fund research for information alone," explains Dr Roestorf. "We fund research that leads to further impact, such as increased funding, new services and policy change.

"We ask questions about the proposed research, such as how it meets the community need and priorities, what the risks and benefits are, and the wider impact of the research or proposed solution beyond our involvement in the project."

ASAN stresses autism research should "always be community-based participatory research".

"It should be led by autistic scientists," they write. "The

scientists doing the research should listen to the autistic community [...] There should be a diverse group of autistic people advising the scientists who do this research."

For NAS, the involvement of autistic people in the research is essential. "Often, the role of us being involved in research is to help facilitate that, so we know when that is good, but we think participation is vital," says Nicholls. "Then there are some particular kinds of interventions that we probably just wouldn't get involved in, either because we don't think they're appropriate, or because we don't have the skills."

He goes on to tell me that these include genetic studies, research that tests behaviour in animals to project the results onto autistic people, and pharmacological interventions – the latter of which is "really not our space".

"Where a potential exception could be is if it's a study relating to a pharmacological intervention for something that isn't autism," adds Nicholls. "So, if it were, for example, 'how well do antidepressants support autistic people who also have depression, do they work differently?'... We're not involved in a study like that, but theoretically, that is a question that we would think would be important to answer.

"And does it benefit autistic people? Does it help inform better support?" he continues. "Is it going to improve people's lives, day to day, across those life challenges – education, employment, health inequality, mental health, medical care? Those are really important things, I think."

A lot of these are, of course, social issues. Many of the challenges in such environments pertain to institutions, attitudes and infrastructure. A large proportion of disabled people – including autistic people – subscribe to the notion that it's these areas that 'disable' them.

Many charities also support the social model of disability, not least because it's far more logical and practical to call for society to change its perceptions around disability and improve physical environments for disabled people, than having to force the disabled people to constantly adjust themselves to the inaccessible world around them. As Nicholls says in reference to the views of NAS, "today's society needs to do a lot to change – this shouldn't be about changing autistic people".

Apply this to research, and you have the studies that take a more biomedical, genetic approach – as explored in previous chapters – and the research that dives into more social model thinking with access to services, for example.

"We do need both approaches," argues Dr Roestorf. "Medical research into treatments for anxiety is essential, but it absolutely has to involve autistic people to create solutions that work for them and meet a diverse range of needs. You can improve the drug and therapy options available on a medical level but that will only make a difference to people's lives if the healthcare system is accessible, and if society is enabling to autistic people.

She continues: "Research can ensure that every neurodivergent person has a personalized profile of their strengths and difficulties. Then, services can organize support around what each individual needs, rather than some overgeneralized, inaccurate and harmful stereotypes about autism or ADHD."

Dr Roestorf also explains that Autistica doesn't fund biological or genetic research, but acknowledges that a "nuanced debate" about its place in the wider autism research industry is important: for example, in terms of autistic people with epilepsy, for whom standard epilepsy treatments are "extremely ineffective", with "too many" individuals dying every year as a result of medical professionals not knowing "how to treat their unique form of seizures".

ASAN makes a different argument. "Genetic research should play a much smaller role in autism research," they write in a document detailing their stance on research into autism.[5]

---

5   Autistic Self Advocacy Network (n.d.).

"Instead, more funding should go to research about services, autism across the lifespan, and other research that the autistic community supports.

"Autism research should study things that are important to autistic people," they stress. "It should study things that can help us right now, instead of trying to 'cure' or stop autism in the future."

They go on to write: "[Our] ultimate goal is for autism research to help end ableism and discrimination towards autistic people. We want research to focus on improving autistic people's lives and the society we live in. We want research to focus on changing the social attitudes that negatively affect autistic people every day.

"We do not want research to focus on changing autistic people to make us 'less autistic' or 'more ready' to fit into a society which rejects us," they state.

Of course, as has been made clear at many points throughout this book, there is a wide range of terminology surrounding autism research and disability, on which academics and advocates will have different opinions.

"The language of research does not match the language of the community and how we would tend to talk about things," Nicholls explains. "Sometimes, I think that's the important role of a charity, to help do the interpretation and work with the academics. If we're involved in research, we think there are noble intentions. We think there's a good reason to do it, and we'd be like, 'a good way to talk about it so people aren't worried about it or concerned about it is this'.

"Because it's not just a cosmetic thing – that you're using the language that [autistic people use] – it's about respect. That's really important that people get to see [this]."

Charities serve as a translator, almost. They take the often formal and intense language of academia and condense it into practical and accessible information, to be used by the organization itself and autistic advocates. Where autism research may be impersonal, charities can work to make it more individualistic, and in doing so, it helps them with their own objectives.

The idea of translating studies is referenced by Autistica when I ask Dr Roestorf where she sees autism research heading in the future. "We look to go beyond simply communicating about the projects we fund," she tells me. "Through identifying, translating and applying research findings for different audiences, we help to ensure that evidence-based solutions are made available to everyone."

She also calls upon researchers to ask more questions prior to beginning their studies, listing a few examples. "Why is this important? How will this change lives? Is there evidence of community need? How can I involve a representative group of autistic people? What will happen after my study finishes? How can I share the results to make a difference?

"These are all questions we expect our applicants to have answered before they approach us for funding, and other funders should do the same – and, broadly, they do," continues Dr Roestorf. "If we have good-quality research we can really start to make progress for autistic people. Bad research wastes money, time and destroys trust and can in some cases lead to poor or even harmful recommendations."

Nicholls' answer is hopeful. "I think the trajectory of autism research is pointing in the right direction," he says, "and I think with greater awareness and understanding in society – increased focus, increased appetite for academics to do research about issues that are important to autistic people – I think we're heading in the right direction.

"I think that we need to still see more improvement of involvement of [autistic] people in [studies], making sure it's right from the start – from design through to publication," he continues. "We'd like to see more academics who are autistic themselves, as well. I think that would be really, really positive, and I would like to see a research community that is thinking hard about the language that it uses to communicate – to itself do some of the work of translating and thinking about things from its academic language, through to the language that everyday people expect and will understand, because I think that's really important. I think it demonstrates a level of respect and empathy that would also help with research being well received."

Although it remains a developing field, Nicholls believes autism research has still come a very long way. "[That is] probably due to a lot of much more progressive thinkers in the last 10 to 15 years than it was before, which is good," he says. "That's not saying there isn't still a way to go. I think that attitude has started to change, and also, there's quite a lot of autistic academics involved in research now, which I think is hugely positive."

Just as much as charities translate autism studies for a more general audience, they can challenge the language used in terms of the message it could potentially convey.

"It's important to say, where we think a narrative is not aligned with our views around autism understanding and acceptance [...] then we'll say it," Nicholls adds. "I think that's an important role for us as well, because how can we seek to speak alongside families and autistic people unless we do that?"

The potential is promising. A growing number of autistic academics are carrying out research the community wants to see, and challenging studies inside the industry that lack significant benefits to their participants. Together with charities scrutinizing narratives on an external level, a possible pathway towards shifting the focus in autism research to more beneficial conversations seems within reach, with improved trust and relations following suit.

However, one practice – tied so closely to autism research – could well be holding that progress back, until the industry is ready to confront all of its uncomfortable truths.

Chapter 8

'FIXED'

Rather poetically, there is a theory that suggests the narrative around autism cures, interventions or 'fixes' are, themselves, fixed. In 2021, autistic educator and researcher Robin Roscigno, together with academic and author Alicia Broderick, established the notion of an "autism industrial complex" (AIC), with the latter publishing a book expanding upon the theory in January 2022.

It was, however, a TEDx talk by Roscigno the year before that I found to be the most enlightening and accessible discussion of the matter (both in terms of finding and understanding the information). It follows a similar narrative to the military industrial complex – the concept long associated with US president Dwight D. Eisenhower which concerns the influence of weapons manufacturers on policymakers to secure more arms sales, and the generation of public fear around national security to increase the pressure from the electorate.

"In the autism industrial complex," Roscigno explains, "the business is autism services and interventions, and the social system that it runs on is also built on fear – specifically parental fear. The more scared you are of autism, the more money you're going to spend to try and fix it."

She cites harmful ABA therapy as one example of the

interventions offered – a procedure interrogated further in this chapter, but that has been found, in some forms, to cause severe psychological pain to those who have been subjected to it. "Spending is increasing," she states, "but autistic people are not reaping the benefits." It is instead, Roscigno and Broderick argue, the AIC that benefits.

Its 'operators' are clearly defined by the duo's 2021 paper 'Autism, Inc.: The Autism Industrial Complex', published in the *Journal of Disability Studies in Education*. The authors point to non-autistic parents of autistic children, Autism Speaks and, perhaps more importantly in the context of this book, "academy behaviourists" – that is, those with "PhDs in behavioral psychology, teaching at institutions of higher education and publishing studies and position papers in peer-reviewed scientific journals".

Upon watching Roscigno's TEDx video, it's easy to see how the AIC theory interconnects with ideas put forward by Dr Botha and Dr Cage (see Chapter 3); in particular, in terms of the benefits to some researchers of dehumanizing autistic people in research, and seeing autism as an amorphous condition separate from the individual, which it very much isn't.

Roscigno even alludes to the aforementioned "I Am Autism" video by Autism Speaks in saying "many successful funding campaigns have been built" on the idea of autism as a kidnapper or "thief robbing their children".

To separate autism from the person is to allow for little to no co-production with the community; to centre the non-autistic researcher and their legacy; and, in the case of the AIC, to make it easier to produce harmful research – research that only serves to spread a narrative of fear, or of autism being some "economic burden".

As Roscigno states brilliantly towards the end of her TEDx talk, "no one benefits from your fear of autism – except the people who want to sell you the antidote". Even then, that "antidote" isn't the right one. The correct approach is about acceptance.

The very antithesis, then, of what ABA is about. The practice relies on a punishment and reward model whereby undesired autistic behaviours are discouraged in favour of more neuro-typical-presenting mannerisms. The act of 'putting on' a more 'non-autistic' persona voluntarily as an autistic person is known as masking, and it's exhausting. When such a process is carried out under duress and a system of punishment, the impact is significant.

While the industry has sought to move away from and no longer align itself with the "restrictive or punishment-based procedures" of 50 years ago (the Ethics Code from the Behavior Analyst Certification Board, or BACB, in effect from January 2022, requires applicants and certificants to "do no harm" and only carry out said procedures when "less intrusive means" have not produced the desired results[1]), no description of the intervention known as ABA is as explicit and sinister as that given by Lovaas – dubbed the "father" of the practice – in an interview from 1974.

"Spank them, and spank them good," Lovaas tells Paul Chance of *Psychology Today*, when asked how to eliminate "aberrant" social behaviours in autistic children. "They bite you and you just turn them over your knee and give them one good whack on the rear and that pretty well does it. This is what we do best; we are very good at controlling these kinds of behaviours. This is also the way we handle self-destructive behaviour."

He goes on to share details of one child he treated named Beth, who was exhibiting such behaviour in the form of hitting herself, to which he responded by hitting her on her backside. In nauseating, fatphobic remarks, he said he had an "easy target", but that her actions stopped for "about 30 seconds". He "felt

---

1   Behavior Analyst Certification Board (2020).

guilty" at the pause, but also "felt great" – before the self-harm started again and Lovaas "really laid it on her".

"I let her know that there was no question in my mind that I was going to kill her if she hit herself once more, and that was pretty much it," he continued. "She hit herself a few times after that, but we had the problem licked."

In the publicly available excerpt, containing an interview and profile of Lovaas, Chance insists "nothing could be further from the truth" in terms of claims his interviewee enjoys abusing and shocking autistic children, yet the aforementioned quote would suggest otherwise. His glee at harming Beth demonstrates a certain kind of sadism, however you try to frame it or justify it (Chance argued that Lovaas believed restraining autistic children to a bed and "[letting] them vegetate" was far more sadistic).

Lovaas is reported to have told a journalist for *Los Angeles Magazine* that he could have turned Adolf Hitler into a "nice man" had he been brought to UCLA aged four or five.[2] According to sources cited by Silberman in *Neurotribes*, Lovaas subjected two children to sounds "'well over 100' decibels" (exposure to noises exceeding 85 decibels for a long period of time risks causing permanent hearing loss), and claimed it was "a pleasure to work with a child who is on mild food deprivation".

Perhaps unsurprisingly, interpretations of Lovaas' papers also present him as another autism researcher sensitive to scrutiny of his studies – understandably so, one might say, when the go-to reaction upon learning about ABA and its extreme procedures was probably one of consternation. As then PhD candidate Rua M. Williams writes in a 2018 paper: "Whenever criticised for these techniques, Lovaas would expose his particular brand of benevolent cruelty. 'While the use of electric shock on individuals with intellectual delays issues may seem

---

2   Zarembo (2012).

inhumane or archaic, its effectiveness in changing behaviour should not be disputed.' Despite his bravado, Lovaas seemed particularly self-conscious of these critiques."

It's easy to see why, given that the abuse of autistic children is quite the charge rallied against him. Clearly, painting ABA as a loving act to rid an autistic child of an amorphous autism, separate from the individual, would be one way of preventing the technique from being shunned as the torture it so evidently was.

It is just one contradiction found in the article. Lovaas explains that he learned "if you treat these kids like patients, you are finished" and that you have to "treat [autistic children] like people". Yet, in that same discussion, he claims one must "start pretty much from scratch when you work with an autistic child".

"You have a person in the physical sense – they have hair, a nose and a mouth – but they are not people in the psychological sense," he suggested, in utterly dehumanizing comments. "One way to look at the job of helping autistic kids is to see it as a matter of constructing a person. You have the raw materials, but you have to build the person."

In a way that is incredibly frustrating, Lovaas at one point seems so close to having an epiphany about the social model of disability. "If you handle things correctly," he states, "you can make a blind or deaf child look very nearly normal. All you have to do is figure out how to make his environment instructive. That's what we do with autistic children."

If only that translated to an approach whereby changes to one's environment concerned increasing accommodations for autistic people, and tackling ableist attitudes. Instead, Lovaas pioneered a practice still used today, with catastrophic consequences.

In fact, a 2018 study by Californian researcher Henny Kupferstein found evidence of increased symptoms of post-traumatic stress disorder (PTSD) in autistic people exposed to ABA. More specifically, after 460 respondents completed an online survey, almost half (46%) of those who had experienced ABA "met the diagnostic threshold for PTSD".

Rather predictably, researchers who "provide or have provided ABA-based intervention" for autistic individuals contest this finding, with representatives from the Autism Special Interest Group in California concluding Kupferstein's research contained "several methodological and conceptual flaws". These included "leading questions used within a non-validated survey, [a] failure to confirm diagnosis, and [an] incomplete description of interventions".[3]

Even so, the potential long-term damage caused by ABA to autistic recipients does not, tragically, stop at possible PTSD symptoms. Maria Scharnke is convinced an "ABA-style speech therapy" she received, which she assumes was to regulate her tone of voice, "pushed" her into being non-speaking "a lot more often than I would have been otherwise".

"I didn't think there was anything wrong with the way I spoke," she explains, "but apparently there was, and if I couldn't mask it up, then the only way not to mask up would be to not speak. So I sort of drilled that into myself."

Ira Kraemer adds: "Basically, you're asking autistic people to seem less autistic, or seem neurotypical. People argue about, 'well, ABA is different now and all this stuff and it's better and there's no punishment anymore'. My argument is that it's not about how you do it – you can do it in any way you want, you can do it with less overt punishment, you can do it with rewards – but at the end of the day, you're asking an autistic kid to pretend to be a neurotypical kid.

"It doesn't really matter what it looks like," they continue, "because the goal is to fit in, and that hurts autistic people."

Meanwhile, a 2019 review article by Sandoval-Norton, Shkedy and Shkedy at the Alternative Teaching Strategy Center – also

---

3   Leaf et al. (2018).

in California – lists several other potential issues: "Compliance, learned helplessness, food/reward-obsessed, magnified vulnerabilities to sexual and physical abuse, low self-esteem, decreased intrinsic motivation, robbed confidence, inhibited interpersonal skills, isolation, anxiety, suppressed autonomy, prompt dependency, adult reliance, etc. continue to be created in a marginalized population who are unable to defend themselves."

This assessment was branded an "inaccurate, pejorative attack" on a treatment which has been "vetted for effectiveness, met that challenge, and stands as a very strong signal of hope for families impacted by ASD" by Gorycki, Ruppel and Zane at the University of Kansas' Department of Applied Behavioral Science. Their 2020 paper, while acknowledging ABA is "not perfect", tackles five main criticisms made by the Californian researchers. This includes what is arguably the main point of contention: that the practice is "unethical and abusive".

"It could not be clearer that the ethical code mandates behaving in a way to maximize benefit and minimize harm," they write, referencing the aforementioned code established and maintained by the BACB. "Practicing outside one's scope is unethical. Practicing incompetently is unethical. Instead, behavior analysts create treatment plans based on the client's needs, as dictated by the client and his/her significant others."

They continue: "The evolution of the ABA ethical code has put in place fundamental guidelines to prevent abuse. A primary goal of ABA treatment is to protect the well-being of individuals and in doing so, the treatment focus is individualized, allowing individuals to learn the necessary skills to develop the most independence."

In 2021, the authors of the 2019 California paper – Aileen Herlinda Sandoval-Norton, Gary Shkedy and Dalia Shkedy – issued a rebuttal to this response to their criticisms.[4] Replying to

---

4   Shkedy, Shkedy and Sandoval-Norton (2021).

the question of whether ABA is ethical, they pointed out that "the issue is not whether or not ABA therapists follow their own ethics code; the issue is the ethical scope of the practice of ABA".

They expand upon this in a later paragraph, breaking it down into three areas: "(1) what behaviour is inherent and appropriate, (2) what expertise is required to make such a determination, and (3) what expertise is required to recognize when the treatment is actually causing harm. In dealing with human beings, it is unethical to make an arbitrary decision on what is an appropriate behaviour, without understanding the long-term ramifications of attempting to change that behaviour."

This brings us to a fact clearly explained by these academics: the necessary accreditations and qualifications do not refer explicitly to a degree or any specific learning on autism. One website cited by Shkedy et al. in 2021 notes that one route is a graduate degree on a subject such as "education" or "behaviour analysis". A review of the accredited universities and their courses listed on the Association for Behavior Analysis International (ABAI) Accreditation Board's website shows programmes concerning behavioural analysis, counselling, psychology and special education. Not one of the bachelors, masters or doctoral courses explicitly mentioned 'autism' in its title.

"This single fact necessarily leads to at least the vast majority of ABA therapists practicing out of their scope," Shkedy et al. explain. "We are unaware of any other profession or circumstance where it is considered ethical to not study anything about the manifestation or circumstances of a condition, and then attempt to treat it. Moreover, it is negligent, dangerous, and malpractice for any professional or paraprofessional to claim expertise and implement interventions for a group they have not vigorously studied."

The paper's overall conclusion is damning. "Research in ABA continues to neglect the structure of the autistic brain, the overstimulation of the autistic brain, the trajectory of child development, or the complex nature of human psychology, as all of these factors were ignored in the response [by the Kansas academics] and are ignored in ABA practice itself," they write. "Providing a treatment that causes pain in exchange for no benefit, even if unknowingly, is tantamount to torture and violates the most basic requirement of any therapy: to do no harm."

Then there's the problem with understanding, accepting and acting upon criticism and scrutiny, which underscores a serious issue with positive progression in the autism research industry. "If paraprofessionals and professionals refuse to engage in critical thinking, refuse to become experts at the thing they treat, continue to practice outside of scope, and continue to ignore pertinent research," Shkedy et al. write, "the future of autism and other conditions ABA professes to treat is very bleak."

Studies also indicate the ABA industry has an honesty problem as well. A 2021 tally by Bottema-Beutel and Crowley of conflict of interest (COI) disclosures in a year's worth of articles about ABA autism intervention strategies, with a particular focus on "researcher employment as an ABA clinical provider or a training consultant to ABA clinical providers", found that 84% of studies reviewed had at least one author with this specific COI. The troubling reality though, noted by the Boston College authors, was that only 2% of studies disclosed such a COI. Not just that, but for 87% of studies with statements where no COIs were declared, authors *did* in fact have a conflict of interest in relation to clinical or training consultancy.

Transparency is integral to trust, and yet this is an intervention and area of autism research that lacks the suitable qualifications, valuable accountability, or an appropriate level of respect for individuals subjected to the practice.

While ABA continues to be studied in academia and practised in the wider autism industry, will trust in autism research always be an issue?

"Frankly, yes, I think it probably is," replies Dr Morénike

Giwa Onaiwu. "I think that the approach that some people are taking isn't addressing the elephant in the room. So there'll be people saying, 'well, yes, old ABA used to be problematic, but now this, this, this and the other', and that's not addressing some of the present concerns that people have. That isn't to negate those problematic things in the past that may not manifest the same way, although some of them do, but there's a lot of issues."

As a brief aside, "old ABA" has become a shorthand for earlier incarnations of the practice that relied on "punishments like yelling, hitting and most controversially electroshocks", as Liz Tung writes for the Philadelphia-focused news outlet WHYY in October 2022. It's a way in which the industry has sought to distance itself from past behaviour and move towards a more "compassionate application" of ABA in ways which are – per ABAI – "ethical, compassionate, and do no harm".

Dr Giwa Onaiwu continues: "So people are basically looking at, 'oh, well let's not use ABA to diminish autistic people's stereotypy or what have you, or let's not push it against someone's will, let's not use terminology they don't like. Basically, let's do ABA, but let's just do ABA lite, let's make it nicer.' That's not addressing the concerns that people have, like it'd be better for a person to get, I guess, a finger amputated than an arm. I mean, that's an improvement, but harm has taken place."

Noor Pervez of ASAN says there's two factors that determine the level of trust in an industry which still practises ABA. "The first one is whether the research community continues to centre and focus on and promote, frankly, a lot of the root behaviourism around ABA," he says. "Currently, fundamentally, it does – that's a pipeline that's kind of circular. A lot of people who are entering research are coming from the ABA space and vice versa, so there's a lot under that.

"The other very large chunk of that is whether or not, at the root of it, there's that shift towards autistic people being the target audience, being who research is for, when it's about us," Pervez continues, "because I don't think those two changes can happen independently of each other. Once you treat autistic people fundamentally as the experts on our own experiences and as the people who need to be there from the beginning to make sure your research is worth anything [...] it suddenly becomes very difficult to see treating us as anything else, as an acceptable barrier of entry to research, I think."

Of course, there are multiple stakeholders interested in the practice of ABA, each with their own approach. "I feel like autistic people are going to continue to not feel listened to, continue to feel frustrated and concerned," says Dr Giwa Onaiwu, "and I think parents are going to continue to be confused and then defensive, and I think it will [continue to happen] until we all kind of sit down and talk about what it is that we're really talking about.

"I think [people] need to understand what ABA is," they go on to add, "as some of the arguments that I think autistic people make about ABA – while well intended – don't help the cause, because some of them are saying things inaccurately or misrepresenting it. I think on the other side, people need to realize the legitimacy of people's lived experiences, who've been harmed by ABA and then realize that even the 'good ABA' could still be problematic."

There's also an element of nuance around ABA which is highlighted by Dr Giwa Onaiwu in a series of tweets posted in January 2022. "I'm not going to begrudge a struggling single Black mom who reluctantly enrols her child in ABA out of acquiescence knowing [if] she hadn't, she'd probably have CPS [child protective services] at her door," she wrote.

During our conversation, I ask her to elaborate further. "I think that what autistic people – especially white ones – fail to realize is there's so much of our lives as Black autistics that's ABA already, that ABA is the least of our worries," they explain. "We have to do things that we hate, that are the lesser of two evils, to survive, not because we want to, but because we have no other alternatives. I didn't want to sit my sons down and have a talk with them about why you're Black and you're assigned male at birth and you're disabled, so you can't do this and you can't do this because you're seen as a threat, you no longer have the protection of youth. I didn't want to have that conversation with my child. It's an emotionally damaging thing to have to tell a child, that [...] you can't do this, but I had to, that's life. I did it whether I wanted to or not.

"So this isn't so alien to us, ABA," she continues. "OK, you learn to speak like this, make eye contact, basically break off some pieces of yourself, compromise some things about yourself, not because you want to but for survival purposes in a world that doesn't care about you. That's our reality."

Dr Giwa Onaiwu does, however, stress that if it's possible for a family to try something else other than ABA, then they should do that. "If you're privileged enough to be able to do a more neurodiversity-affirming approach or home-school or do whatever it is that you can do, please do so. But if you've got to go with this – if you're risking your child's custody being taken away because you're not 'using the gold standard of healthcare, medical neglect' – then just be very involved. Be that parent, make it the lesser of two evils. Try to make sure that you watch and you're involved and you can mitigate the damage.

"It's not between a good choice and a bad choice," they go on to add. "It's between two bad choices, and I think people need to be cognizant of that. Until there's an alternative for parents, to our families, then this is what's going to happen, and ABA programmes are everywhere."

While ABA continues to harm the reputation *of* and level of trust *in* autism research, one particular case has attracted widespread condemnation over its use of what it calls "contingent skin shock [CSS] for severe problem behaviour", using a device known as a "graduated electronic decelerator".

The example in question is the Judge Rotenberg Education-al Center (JRC), a residential school in Massachusetts, whose decision to use shocks as "aversives" borrows straight from the ABA "reward and punishment" playbook, and has led to a tireless campaign from autistic advocates against the school organized under #StopTheShock on social media.

The JRC says, "positive-only educational and treatment procedures" are used first before considering aversives, and claims that if they are applied to a student's treatment programme, then there are multiple safeguards in place. A policy document on the school's website lists more than 20, including: parental consent forms every year ("no aversive is employed without prior, written informed consent", which can be withdrawn at any time); a meeting to discuss adding an aversive to the student's Individualized Education Programme and annual follow-ups; reviews by the Massachusetts Probate Court, independent clinicians and physicians; and oversight by human rights and peer review committees.[5]

The school adds there's also a legal process with the Probate Court, involving a court-appointed attorney to represent a student's best interests, before a judge rules on a proposed treatment plan. The opposing counsel, the JRC writes, can "object to the treatment plan [...] at any time".

As for parental review, the JRC document explains parents can monitor treatment through a website, which details "the number of aversives administered each day, what behaviours they were administered for, and the progress the student is making". Further monitoring also comes in the form of a 24/7 "digital video monitoring system".

Then there's safeguards around the application of the aversives, and medical care. "Direct care staff do body checks on all students each morning and evening," the policy document

---

5   Judge Rotenberg Center (2018).

reads. "All applications of the aversive are reported to nursing staff who do a body check on the student within 24 hours. The electrode site is checked each hour, when the electrode is rotated, and also after each application. Each student receives a complete medical examination at least annually, and is referred to a medical specialist if needed. Nursing care is provided on a 24/7, round-the-clock basis."

It continues: "The number of applications of the skin shock that are used with any student who has skin shock in his/her treatment plan is kept low. The average student receives less than one application per week. If more than one application in any 24-hour period is required, the student's clinician sets the number which may be administered before he or she is notified and gives further approval. This number can be no greater than 10."

Notice how under this specific point, it is not clear as to whether the parent too has a limit before they are notified and have to grant their approval for further applications. Of course, there is the fact they can withdraw consent at any time and have the monitoring tool available to them, but this section of the document does not make clear as to whether a parent is informed of an increase in applications *before* they are applied to their child.

I detail all of the above not only in the interests of presenting the JRC's defence, but also for reference as news reports, video footage and anecdotal evidence call into question the compassionate stance the JRC might have people believe.

First and foremost, there is an understanding among many that self-injurious behaviours (what the JRC describes unhelpfully as "problem behaviour") are actions deployed during moments of distress. To shock, therefore, is to attempt to conceal or suppress that sentiment as much as it does the way in which this is expressed (the physical actions).

This process, of course, is exactly the same as other manifestations of ABA, which too deal in the act of enforced masking or suppression. Sensitive and supportive alternatives to this torture – centred in local communities – exist, and as ASAN notes: "people with the exact same disabilities as the people at the JRC get support that helps them with the exact same problems, without aversives".[6] There is, in other words, another way.

Yet the JRC proceeds with the application of electric shock treatments, and the most harrowing story to emerge from the Massachusetts institution concerned then 18-year-old Andre McCollins, a Black autistic teenager who was restrained and electrocuted 31 times in a single day in 2002. Horrifying video footage of McCollins screaming in pain, of which the JRC's attorneys tried and failed to convince a judge to block the release, was made available to the public a decade later and can still be located online at the time of writing.

A description of the video played during the 2012 court case – which concluded with the JRC and mother Cheryl McCollins agreeing to a confidential settlement – was given by Boston25 News at the time. They write of Andre staying still despite being asked several times to remove his coat, before being shocked and falling to the floor. He's then restrained face-down by staff.

According to Jennifer Gonnerman, writing in the *New York* magazine in 2012, the reason given to Ms McCollins for the extensive number of shocks was due to her son "tensing up" his body – an action considered an "unhealthy behaviour".

Ms McCollins' testimony during the court hearing is just as devastating. "I never signed up for him to be tortured, terrorized and abused," she said to members of the jury. "I had no idea – no idea – that they tortured the children in the school."

She continued to talk of the detrimental impact the "treatment" had had on her son, describing him being in a "catatonic" state when visiting him three days after the horrific incident.

---

6   Autistic Self Advocacy Network (2023).

"I couldn't turn Andre's head to the left or the right. He was just staring straight. I took my hands and went like this," she explained, waving her hands in front of her eyes. "He didn't blink."

A children's hospital diagnosed Andre with acute stress response, and tragically, he's not the only former student of the JRC to be left with psychological scars from his time at the institution.

Rico Torres was just eight when he was shocked for the first time. In an interview with NBC News in 2021, aged 24, he said he now lives with "a fear of authority [and] a fear of being controlled", which causes him to panic when he is "presented with either".[7]

While Andre's fear in the traumatic environment reportedly caused him to tense up, and thus receive further shocks, Rico spoke of being shocked because he "didn't wake up" from his sleep, only to be electrocuted again when this led to him wetting the bed.

Another shattering trauma response: "My pain tolerance has gone to the point that I can't really feel anything," Rico reveals. "I get tattoos as a reminder of it. Sometimes all I crave is pain."

This is torture, and I say this not for dramatic effect, but rather as a statement of fact. In 2013, the then Special Rapporteur on Torture for the United Nations, Juan Méndez, concluded in a report that "the rights of the students of the JRC subjected to Level III Aversive Interventions by means of electric shock and physical means of restraints have been violated under the UN Convention against Torture and other international standards." His report also called for a "prompt and impartial investigation" by the US government into the practices.

The JRC has dismissed claims that the UN classes the use of CSS as torture, saying Méndez "released a statement based on a false report submitted by an advocacy group".[8]

---

7   McFadden, Monahan and Kaplan (2021).

8   Judge Rotenberg Center (n.d.).

When approached for a response to this claim in November 2023, Méndez said over email that he stands by what was published about the JRC when he was the UN Special Rapporteur on Torture.

"Like in all cases of individual complaints," he writes, "we received the information originally from a human rights organization. We then pursued the case with corroborating sources. We were invited by the Center to visit, but had to include such visit in a general country visit to the US to include prisons as well as other places of deprivation of freedom; the general visit did not take place because the US did not guarantee acceptable terms of reference.

"Nevertheless, what we criticized about physical and other restrictions applied at JRC merited our report because they constituted torture or cruel, inhuman or degrading treatment under relevant international standards of human rights."

The JRC should be careful when talking of false reports, though, as one made to the institution in 2007 further cements the school's reputation for harming autistic and other disabled individuals. Back then, one former JRC resident pretended to be a member of the school's quality control department and managed to convince staff members to deliver at least 70 shocks to one student, and 29 shocks to another.[9]

Amid the outcry over this incident, the school's founder Matthew Israel was indicted over allegations he ordered staff to destroy video evidence of the night in question. In 2011, Ed Pilkington reported in *The Guardian* that Israel had been forced to depart the JRC and serve five years' probation, as part of an agreement with prosecutors. Martha Coakley, then the attorney general for Massachusetts, is quoted by the newspaper as saying: "Dr Israel then attempted to destroy evidence of the events and mislead investigators, and that conduct led to his indictments

9   Borenstein (2013).

today. Today's action removes Dr Israel from the school and should ensure better protection for students in the future."

Israel's defence attorney, Max Stern, insisted his client was "not guilty of any offence" in response to the indictment. The local news website Patch reported that Stern said: "[Israel] should not have been indicted. The claim that he tried to cover up a crime is entirely without substance."[10]

Fast forward to 2020, and the Food and Drugs Administration (FDA) banned the use of the electronic devices behind the shocks as something that poses an "unreasonable and substantial risk of illness or injury that cannot be corrected or eliminated through new or updated device labelling".[11] This was challenged by the JRC a year later, and their petition was successful, as the US Court of Appeals for the District of Columbia Circuit ruled the FDA's ban was one placed on medicinal practice, which is beyond the agency's remit.[12]

In a significant development in November 2022, the ABAI published a statement strongly opposing the use of CESS [contingent electric skin shock] "under any condition". They cite concerns relating to "human rights, insufficient evidence demonstrating the efficacy of CESS compared to alternative treatments, a lack of social validity, and consistent cultural considerations being raised by individuals and organizations worldwide".

While they note CESS can "suppress behavior", they add it doesn't address its *function*, and instead the emotional side-effects and "likelihood of trauma" could get in the way of adopting "adaptive behavioral repertoires".[13] On the topic of ethics, they bring up the Hippocratic Oath's "do no harm" pledge, as

---

10   Gentes-Hunt (2011).

11   Food and Drug Administration (2020).

12   United States Court of Appeals for the District of Columbia Circuit (2021).

13   Association for Behavior Analysis International (2022).

well as the considerations around protecting the welfare of individuals and securing consent and assent. Whatever form it takes – be it a shock or another "milder" repressive approach – the use of punishment in ABA will always be counteractive to the ethical principles that uphold healthcare.

Just a month later, another blow to the JRC was delivered in the form of an omnibus bill signed by US President Joe Biden. A report from the Committee on Energy and Commerce in 2022 explains rather helpfully the changes and new measures afforded to the FDA – more so than the congress.gov website.

Referencing the aforementioned ban which was overturned by the District of Columbia Court of Appeals, the committee's report reads: "FDA's ban applied to shock devices intended for use on a particularly vulnerable patient population – individuals who engage in self-injurious and aggressive behaviour, conditions that present in individuals with intellectual and developmental disabilities such as autism spectrum disorder, Down's syndrome, and Tourette's syndrome.

"FDA determined that these devices intended for this use present an unreasonable and substantial risk of illness or injury based on the serious risks they pose, the inadequacy of data to show effectiveness, and the positive benefit-risk profiles of behavioral and pharmacological alternatives developed in recent decades to treat patients with these conditions," it continues. It notes that medical literature has revealed that the devices carried risks of tissue damage, depression and PTSD, among other physical and psychological harms. It said the FDA engaged in an "extensive process" with stakeholders before making the ban, and that the new rules under the Food and Drug Amendments of 2022 would "reinstitute this ban" without extra proceedings which would use up time and resources.

"Electrical stimulation devices that apply a noxious electrical stimulus to a person's skin intended to reduce or cease self-injurious behaviour or aggressive behaviour are deemed to be banned devices," Section 811(c) states. Zoe Gross, director of advocacy at ASAN, described the legislation as a "step forward", telling the Disability Scoop website it "opens the door for FDA to pass another ban without fear that it will be struck down on the same grounds [as the previous ban overturned by the DC court]".[14]

In September 2023, a judgment from the Supreme Judicial Court of Massachusetts ruled that the state's Department of Developmental Services cannot "prospectively ban the use of level three aversives for all new patients [at the JRC...] without running afoul" of a 1987 decree which includes a requirement for both the department and JRC to "act in good faith".

"If the department seeks to get out from under the decree," the ruling reads, "it must either wait for a legislative solution, provide more robust evidence that electric skin shock is outside the standard of care than the record it relied upon in 2016, or establish an ongoing record of good faith regulatory conduct toward JRC."[15]

And so, the fight to ban the devices from being used on any autistic person, at the time of writing, continues.

From Lovaas to the JRC, all of it makes for distressing reading. Part of what's so horrifying about it all is that these practices and ideologies are not insidious, despite what the widespread condemnation of eugenics might have us believe about it being confined to society's fringes.

The outbreak of coronavirus around the world is an event seared into the global consciousness, and it exposed a passive, ableist disregard towards the wellbeing of disabled people – both in the more conspiratorial, right-wing circles of the general public and, indeed, government. In the UK, the Conservative Party's failings contributed to disabled people

---

14   Diament (2023).
15   Supreme Judicial Court of Massachusetts (2023).

making up 60% of COVID deaths between January and November 2020.[16] Whether it's the supposed preservation of civil liberties in the fight to remain free from masks or lockdowns, or the elimination of a supposed economic "burden" associated with a particular condition such as autism, disabled people's rights are so easily superseded by a purpose considered higher than that of protecting or supporting an oppressed minority.

Even a political body as established as the European Commission is happy to contribute financially to a study which explicitly wants to work towards "disease interception" in relation to autism – to the tune of €14.2 million, in fact. Coordinated by Italy's Fondazione EBRIS (or the European Biomedical Research Institute of Salerno), the initiative is known as the GEMMA project. Details on both the European Commission website[17] and in an article shared by open access publisher MDPI[18] refer to the study seeking to identify biomarkers for "precision treatment and primary prevention" of autism – specifically in relation to "at-risk children".

There's perhaps another, unspoken reason why one has to click to "show the project objective" on the European Commission's webpage on the GEMMA project, because its wording is horrific. If biomarkers are indeed identified through the initiative, and infants with autistic siblings are monitored, then it could contribute to the possibility of being able to "manipulate the microbiota [microorganisms in a particular site]" for "prevention and treatment".[19]

The researchers' reasoning behind exploring autism in detail would be laughable if it wasn't so terrifying. "A large number of individuals are living with ASD," they write, adopting a form of

---

16 Office for National Statistics (2021).
17 Community Research and Development Information Service (2023).
18 Troisi et al. (2020).
19 Community Research and Development Information Service (2023).

person-first language which, as mentioned previously, makes it easier to separate the intrinsic condition of autism as something amorphous. "Thus, ASD is a serious public health concern."

To put it another way, the mere existence of autistic people and their prevalence is an issue. The academics cite several co-morbidities experienced by autistic individuals – ranging from epilepsy and ADHD to "disruptive behaviour" and sleep problems – as concerns, as well as "medical expenditure" for autism being "higher than that for cancer, heart disease and stroke combined".

Comparing a neurological condition to deadly diseases is not only appalling and inappropriate, but fails to acknowledge a significant distinction when it comes to autism. The relevant 2014 study from the London School of Economics, University of Pennsylvania and the Children's Hospital of Philadelphia – complete with its oft-cited £32 billion figure for UK spending on autism care – includes the cost variable of "special education", which can't be applied to cancer, heart disease or stroke.

Upon reading the full text of the study paper – funded by Autism Speaks, by the way – the £32 billion statistic appears to emerge from combining the £29 billion cost from autistic adults with the £3.1 billion cost from autistic children (assuming 40% have an intellectual disability in both groups). If one was to consider a higher prevalence of intellectual disability at 60%, then the cost from autistic adults and children would be £31 billion and £3.4 billion respectively, totalling £34.4 billion.

In other words, the £32 billion estimation may even be lower than the actual amount.

All of this is to say that, so often, a profound economic cost of autism is presented as justification for more radical interventions or even prevention, when the main figure referenced by academics is based on estimations and unfair – or, frankly, inappropriate – comparisons.

To go one step further, Dr Adam Rutherford writes in *Control*, his accessible but otherwise disappointing book on "the dark history and troubling present" of eugenics: "Sometimes debate around such issues talk about the burden on society, or on families, that people with disabilities pose, or that choosing to have a baby with a particular disability increases the sum total of human suffering. I don't think attempts to apply metrics help here at all."[20]

Control also examines the eugenics at the heart of the Nazi regime, and draws attention to comments made about mentally ill individuals – such as those with schizophrenia – by Adolf Hitler in 1933. "It is right that the worthless lives of such creatures should be ended, and that this would result in certain savings in terms of hospitals, doctors and nursing staff."

Disability interventions don't seem so dangerous and problematic when they're buried under pound and dollar signs followed by several zeros. Money, unsurprisingly, is a good distraction.

I say Dr Rutherford's book is disappointing, by the way, because there are multiple missed opportunities to emphasize just how wedded ableism is to eugenics. When Dr Rutherford discusses the ideas of a "well born" individual at the heart of eugenicist ideology; encouraging "the health of individuals in the next generation"; and that no child should be born into pain, he adds that the trouble with such a vision is that it "has always been – and perhaps can never not be – locked in step with deeply illiberal positions".

"Racism, sexism, and classism are inherently built into attempts to make people fitter, happier, more productive," writes Dr Rutherford, failing to acknowledge that ableism also applies to all three of these attempts. Chronically ill people still get asked if they've tried yoga or exercise to alleviate their symptoms (it was only as recently as 2020 that the UK's advisory

---

20 Rutherford (2022).

body NICE issued draft guidance advising against the use of graded exercise therapy for those with chronic fatigue syndrome or myalgic encephalomyelitis – ME for short). Psychological conditions and mental illnesses have to contend with messages of toxic positivity. Disabled people continue to be judged and abused based on their capacity to work.

In one of the many parts of the book where Dr Rutherford emphasizes the strong connection between the scientific and the political, the academic states: "Those criteria that sat in the foundations of eugenics were not absolute metrics of human worth, but were often arbitrary value judgements issued by decree of the powerful. Undesirable, defective, disabled – these are political terms, which change with time, whim and culture."

He's not wrong, but this argument can be developed further. Ultimately a shared but unspoken understanding on what society considers to be "healthy" is no doubt determined by powerful and established institutions, too. Even as a neurological condition, as opposed to a physical one, autism has had to contend with a handful of attempts to subgroup the community – from the outlying condition of Asperger's syndrome differentiating individuals from those with autism spectrum condition (before it was dropped from the DSM diagnostic handbook), to the ongoing debate around a label of "profound autism" and its usage around describing autistic people with high support needs.

Dr Rutherford contests that prenatal screenings are "medical techniques specifically conceived and designed for the alleviation of suffering in individuals", but this again betrays a lack of consideration for the current disability discourse. "Suffering" is just another word determined by authority figures, like "healthy".

Certain academics deal in abstractions, such as the amorphous "autism" and the ambiguous phrase "problem behaviour". Is it any wonder, then, that autistic people – characteristically in favour of clarity and the "black and white" – are so opposed to an industry which still sees some academics operate in such grey areas?

This breakdown of absolutes extends to the language around autism research described previously – some have no doubt capitalized on such ambiguity. If we are to continue to talk about battles over narratives, then the push towards redefining terminology used to oppress autistic people is very much a part of that.

Interventions for autism, whether genetic or behavioural in relation to an individual's environment, seek to change a person at great moral cost, when it is far more cost-effective, ethical and logical to adapt society to be more accommodating. Many studies and practices are focusing on the wrong thing.

Even the Spectrum 10K study talks of "genetically-defined subgroups". Its combination of exploring both the genetic and environmental factors that contribute to autism speaks to the "nature versus nurture" line around how conditions develop – how much does autism come down to biology, and to an individual's environment?

It's largely accepted that autism is primarily genetic, but studies have already explored some environmental factors. Canadian researchers Vinet et al. in 2015 concluded there was an increased risk of a child developing autism if the mother has systemic lupus erythematosus, an autoimmune disease. The same year a study by Zerbo et al. in Philadelphia and Stockholm – funded by Autism Speaks – suggested a pregnant mother hospitalized with an infection may have a higher risk of having an autistic child.

This brings us back to the GEMMA study funded by the European Commission. When considered alongside the practice of ABA, it's possible to see a dual onslaught on autistic people which targets both nature and nurture – an attack on autism before it can develop genetically, and an assault on its traits and its presentation in autistic children in their formative years.

Dr Rutherford bemoans instances where the term "eugenics" has been "thrown around as an insult to scientists who do any work in the field of human or behavioural genetics", yet when ABA as a procedure is performed to falsely encourage uniformity for societal betterment, it sure reads as a modern extension of the eugenicist's way of thinking – even if it's moved away from its original focus on genetics in particular. Even then, that element is picked up by studies such as the GEMMA project – one which Dr Heini Natri argues "violates" the ethical guidelines for research set out by its funder, the European Commission.

Drawing upon the European Charter of Fundamental Rights – specifically Article 3 on the "right to the integrity of the person" – the document notes that "in the fields of medicine and biology, the following must be respected in particular [...] the prohibition of eugenic practices, in particular those aiming at the selection of persons".[21]

Dr Natri also pointed out that as the project – which has the UK, US, Netherlands, Italy, France, Finland and Ireland as national participants – focuses on children "who cannot provide informed consent", there's another issue in relation to respecting "the free and informed consent of the person concerned, according to the procedures laid down by law". It's a point that also makes reference to the Article 3 right to integrity in the aforementioned charter.

Yet despite all this concern, it appears the EU Commission has maintained its support for the GEMMA project, and it's still ongoing at the time of writing.

"GEMMA is focused on the identification of environmental (intestinal microorganisms and their metabolites) and genetic factors which, through epigenetic interaction, could cause autism," Professor Alessio Fasano of the EBRIS Foundation, and

---

21   European Union (2000).

coordinator of the GEMMA project, explained in an unpublished press statement. "The study aims to understand the biological mechanisms of gene-environment interaction but to act *only* on environmental causes (intestinal pathogens), not on genetic ones (besides eugenic manipulation [being] not at all our target, it is also extremely complex to implement in a multifactorial condition like ASD).

"For this purpose," Professor Fasano continued, "GEMMA is developing ad hoc pre-probiotics formulas. Pre-probiotics administration to re-balance a dysbiotic gut microbiota for slowing down/arrest the progression of ASD in newly diagnosed ASD patients, or, even more ambitiously, to intercept the disease in its pre-clinical phase, are the paramount goals of this project."

Though incorrectly viewing autism as a "disease" rather than as a neurological condition is hardly reassuring. Attempts to "slow down", "arrest" or "intercept" autism and/or its progression are just as problematic and alarming as outright prevention, for if there is a concession that such a neurodevelopmental condition such as autism cannot be "cured" – and it cannot – then to halt its development is the next logical step for those who view the disability as inherently negative.

"We understand that some autistic people with a good quality of life believe autism is not something to be 'cured' or prevented but, on the other hand, there are many families with children for whom current treatment options are limited and not efficacious," Professor Fasano added. "These are families that ask for help and are looking for new approaches to improve their children's symptoms and quality of life: GEMMA addresses precisely this subgroup of families. Bottom line: we do not have the ambition to 'eradicate ASD' or impose novel diagnostic and/or therapeutic approaches [on] those ASD subjects that are perfectly OK in managing their condition."

In saying this, then, there's the implication that they very much intend to do this to autistic individuals who are *not* considered to be "managing their condition" to a desired standard, which may well be a roundabout way of referring to autistic people with high support needs ("low functioning"). Even then, informal surveys from Chris Bonnello of the website Autistic Not Weird in 2018 and 2022 – both completed by more than 11,000 people – found that of the respondents who were non-speaking, situationally mute and/or had learning difficulties, the majority said they would disagree or strongly disagree with the statement "if there were a cure for my autism, I would take it".

As explained previously, autistic subgroups are harmful concepts which seriously impact the level of support afforded to autistic individuals. They encourage stigma, and it is not for autism researchers to minimize our lived experiences into a limiting, reductionist box. Understanding and accepting autism is to appreciate the way in which it shapes our lives completely.

Arguably, academia has failed to fully grasp the concepts of neurodiversity and what it is to be neurodivergent. A simple way to distinguish between the two is that an individual can be (neuro)divergent, but not (neuro)diverse. "Neurodivergent" was coined by autistic activist Kassiane Asasumasu, while autistic sociologist Judy Singer is widely credited with introducing the latter term to academia in her 1998 thesis touching upon the "politics of neurodiversity". In the paper, Singer writes that "the 'neurologically different' represent a new addition to the familiar political categories of class/gender/race".[22]

Though in June 2023, it was her comments on the political category of gender that saw Singer receive widespread condemnation and criticism, after penning a number of tweets branded "transphobic" by the autistic community.

In a lengthy blog post published in November 2023, she

---

22 Singer (n.d.).

addressed the backlash by explaining it had occurred to her after she voiced her agreement on Twitter with the claim that "trans women are not women".

She later took to social media to apologize, but this was soon rescinded, writing in the aforementioned November blog post that she took back the apology "because I did not write it in the first place".

The post also saw her state, "I continue to affirm that Trans-women [sic] can never be women and should choose their own name" but that this "does not make me transphobic".

A group of autistic academics later challenged the notion of Singer being the sole originator of the term "neurodiversity", arguing in a March 2024 letter published in *Autism* that the word and theory associated with it actually have several different origins.[23] They claim it was coined collectively.

Let's be clear: a group of people in which each person has a different neurological condition (say autism, ADHD and OCD) is neuro*diverse*, but every single individual is neuro*divergent*. Again, there is the understanding here that every mind is different, but there's a shared "neurological difference" to those who are neurotypical which groups us together.

We've already seen advocates within this book talk of neurodiversity and the need for autism researchers to engage more with this paradigm, which is increasing in popularity. Zachary Williams of INSAR claims that, overall, "the neurodiversity paradigm in broad strokes is very uncontroversial among most researchers". It's only in this chapter and the above paragraphs, however, that I address the concept directly and elaborate on its purpose. Much like Singer herself writes on her website about not offering a definition of neurodiversity in her 1998 thesis, "I thought the meaning [of neurodiversity] was self-evident", but if this book calls on researchers to embrace this paradigm – and

---

23 Botha et al. (2024).

it does – then to be crystal clear on what it means in practice is a basic courtesy.

After all, it's dangerous to be monolithic when imagining the complexity of human psychology, and by subgrouping autistic people, academics disregard autism in its entirety, choosing instead to reduce or generalize our behaviours and perspectives. It is impossible for GEMMA to *only* seek to target select subgroups or demographics of autistic people with preventative or "arrestive" interventions, as there is a commonality within all autistic people (that's rather the point with diagnoses) which would mean it would affect us all.

"Rather," Professor Fasano elaborates, "we want to gain more mechanistic insights to understand why some people develop ASD, why this condition is on the rise, and what can be done to mitigate its impact on the quality of life of ASD subjects and their families."

This, however, contradicts what many believe to be the reason for an increase in the number of diagnoses – namely around a significant boost in awareness and understanding of the condition.

"Then again, GEMMA was approved by an ethics committee," the project coordinator notes, "participation in the project is absolutely on a volunteer basis and therefore only families who freely choose to join the study are participating and can withdraw at any time."

Meanwhile, a European Commission spokesperson tells me over email: "The project GEMMA was submitted to a 2018 call for proposals that generally aimed at reconciling better health and healthy ageing with the need to develop sustainable health and care systems and growth opportunities for health and care related industries. All proposals that had been submitted underwent an evaluation by independent external experts and were scored against the selection and award criteria [of] 'excellence, impact, and quality and efficiency of implementation'.

"Actions carried out under the Horizon 2020 programme have to comply with ethical and research integrity principles, and relevant EU, national and international law," they continue. "The proposal GEMMA was assessed on these ethics requirements and principles before the start of the project."

The statement concludes: "Beneficiaries must carry out the project in compliance with ethical and research integrity principles, including respect for society and research participants. The project is monitored accordingly."

How both the GEMMA project and the practice of ABA (including at the JRC) influence trust in autism research should hopefully be apparent immediately. The pursuit of neurotypical behaviours at the expense of an autistic individual's wellbeing, and the collection of genetic material with the risk of this leading to eradication, are both underpinned by flawed economic purposes. One seeks to monetize "behavioural conditioning" through the Autism Industrial Complex, while the other looks to preserve the public purse.

In this sense, they very much contradict each other (you cannot seek to control the behaviour of a condition you have prevented), and so in addition to being seen by autistic people as eugenicist and pointless expenditure, these practices read as dangerous distractions from far more pressing issues. Co-morbid conditions cannot be explored appropriately on a genetic level when autistic people fear how their DNA will be used, and the much-needed conversations around essential attitudinal changes in society aren't being explored with the appropriate depth, because it's overshadowed by a misplaced desire to correct the individual.

The narrative around 'fixing' autism is predominantly economical, and sometimes even marred by financial irresponsibility. Is it any wonder that this leads one to approach autism research – least of all genetic studies – with so much apprehension and distrust?

Not just that, but when we consider the extent of the financial investment in these studies and practices, then another piece of the puzzle – to use an otherwise problematic metaphor in the context of autism – reveals itself.

Chapter 9

CHEQUES AND BALANCES

I was yet to come across a more perfect representation of research than the rows upon rows of folders adorning the shelves behind Barbara Molony-Oates, as we talked on a video call in October 2022.

The HRA's public involvement manager, who is also autistic, has a role which she says works in two directions. "We work within the HRA, making sure the public have more and more access to how the HRA works," she explains. "The overall intention is to try and help people understand better what the Health Research Authority does, so that they can trust that when we have looked at some research, it's trustworthy – because that's the whole point. Our ID, our whole point of being, is to make it easy for people to do research that people can trust."

Molony-Oates continues: "Therefore, when people don't trust research, it's because they don't know what kind of rigorous testing any sort of NHS research has actually been through. So we're trying to make that a much more open, transparent process, and it's a long road rather than the beginning of a journey," she reveals. "We regularly fail, but we are very open to feedback, and we are on a constant learning process with that."

Then there's the external element of her work, and that isn't without its challenges either. "We want to raise the profile of public involvement in the whole spectrum of the health and social care research area," she says, "and one of the problems we have is that by the time the research application comes to us, a massive amount of work has already been done."

By that, Molony-Oates means the plans are in place, money has been received and a proposal is ready to go, with the HRA being the "last stop gate" before the research has the green light to proceed.

"If they haven't done any public involvement at all, it's really hard for us to say no to the research, because the research is important," she explains. "It's relevant, it's urgent – especially the COVID research, it's really important to get that through. If we had told them to go back to the drawing board and start again with public involvement, that wouldn't have been in the best interest of the public. So we have this really difficult balancing act.

"What we're trying to do is get the message out there earlier in the process, and to try and make sure that if you involve people at the very, very beginning, first of all your research is going to be much more relevant to the actual population that you're working with," Molony-Oates continues. "The problems that researchers get all the time – with recruitment, with objections to research – all those problems can be handled before it even gets going if you involve the right people."

It doesn't help that there's no legal requirement for public involvement in research, though. Ensuring "patients, service users and the public are involved in the design, management, conduct and dissemination of research, unless otherwise justified", is instead encouraged as one of 15 principles listed under the UK's Policy Framework for Health and Social Care Research, a set of responsibilities for researchers which draws upon existing legislation.[1]

---

1   Health Research Authority (2023a).

"The ethics committees don't like approving research where the public involvement hasn't been done," says Molony-Oates. "They really, really don't like it, but they don't have a legal arm to say you *can't* do it, so they have to keep balancing up."

Does she want to see it made a legal requirement? "That would be brilliant," Molony-Oates replies, "but even then, you could insist on it and people can still do tokenistic public involvement. It's the quality of it that we need to work on, and that's going to be a long-term piece of work. We say, 'you have to do public involvement', they say, 'oh, well, we showed the consent form to 20 people and they said it was OK'. They have done some public involvement, but we want proper quality public involvement threaded through research.

"That's going to take a behavioural change, and to change behaviour takes time, but we are 100% committed to it," she says.

So just how receptive are researchers to the idea of increased public involvement? "It's a complete spectrum," reveals Molony-Oates. "So some people go, 'no, I can't do it. That's impossible.' Almost, 'why are you telling me to do that? This is a crucial time, you don't need to do that', and to the opposite end of the spectrum, where they really listen, because our research ethics committees are made up of members of the public, and they're saying, 'this is not ethical to do it this way', and they will then go back and completely revisit their research and take on board that message.

"You get a complete spectrum of responses," she adds, "from very, very reluctant, not very happy about it at all, to 'oh my goodness, yes, we can see how public involvement can make a real difference. Let's do that.'"

The bottom line, Molony-Oates goes on to explain, is that if communities aren't consulted as part of research about them, or feel that they haven't been *meaningfully* consulted, then they won't necessarily engage with the outcomes because they think it doesn't apply to them.

"We saw it with COVID research," she says, "because initially there was a lot of fear and 'mis-stories' about the vaccines and the researchers had to do a lot of backpedalling and a lot of work to build up that trust because they hadn't involved people right at the beginning, so certain communities just didn't trust it."

The impact of the coronavirus pandemic on public involvement was stark. "Before COVID about 80% of the studies that we looked at said that they've done some public involvement at some point, and then when COVID hit that dropped down to 17% really, really quickly," says Molony-Oates. "So we discovered that public involvement wasn't as properly embedded with the research community as we thought it was."

A significant response came in March 2022, when 13 organizations signed a "shared commitment" to greater embed public involvement in research. Alongside the HRA, signatories include Cancer Research UK, Universities UK, the Medicines and Healthcare Products Regulatory Agency (MHRA) and the Association of Medical Research Charities (AMRC).[2]

"Public involvement," it reads, "is important, expected and possible in all types of health and social care research.

"Excellent public involvement is inclusive, values all contributions, ensures people have a meaningful say in what happens and influences outcomes, as set out in the UK Standards for Public Involvement.

"We will: listen to and learn from the people and communities we involve and apply and share that learning; build and share the evidence of how to involve the public and the impact this has; support improvements in equality, diversity, and inclusion in public involvement; promote the UK Standards for Public Involvement," it states.

As an aside, those six UK standards pertain to accessible and inclusive research opportunities; valuable, respectful and

---

2   Health Research Authority (2023b).

productive relationships; support and learning opportunities; public involvement in governance; plain language communications; and sharing the impact of public involvement.[3]

"We need to be saying, you can't just drop it," says Molony-Oates. "You didn't drop your statistician, you didn't drop your methodologist, you can't drop your public involvement. So we need to make this message stronger.

"If they come in in certain routes, they get a really strong message. If they come through the NIHR [National Institute for Health and Care Research], it's obvious. But if they come in through a charity or if they raise the money through business or something like that, it's not so easy.

"We have to speak to organizations and companies that are working internationally as well, so you might get a large, multinational pharmaceutical company coming to us with a research study, and they're based in lots of different countries and we say, 'well, we still want you to do public involvement. We want you to look at the population in the UK, and make sure that the research that you're doing is going to be relevant and applicable and important and acceptable to them.'"

Of course, participation could be a whole lot more diverse, too. "I think we need to make sure that we're including autistic people in the people that we reach out to to get involved," admits Molony-Oates. "Disability itself is underrepresented – in both ethics committees and public involvement. Not necessarily neurodiversity, but definitely like, for example, if you can't hear or if you can't read properly, or if you're blind, it's much more difficult to access documents. If you're dyslexic like me as well, you need printed documents – that means everything takes longer, it's more expensive.

"So including people with disabilities is more difficult, but we want to do it. We're working towards doing it, but we

---

3   UK Standards for Public Involvement (2019).

recognize at the moment that our committees and our volunteers aren't fully diverse.

"Because, you know, if you're going to be giving up a lot of your time and energy to be on a research ethics committee, you have to have the availability of that time," Molony-Oates explains. "You have to be able to read all these complex documents, you have to be able to process that work. As a result, the people who volunteer to do it are people that have a bit of money, they have a bit of time, they have the scientific knowledge. We need to broaden that pool. We need to make that pool wider."

Where chances to participate are advertised has a part to play in that. "The opportunities are open to everybody to be involved in the research committees and the confidential advisory groups, but we only advertise them through LinkedIn and Twitter and things like that – and word of mouth," says Molony-Oates. "I think this is one of the angles that we really need to look at when we're trying to broaden our community – reaching out in other ways, because we are continuously talking to the people that we continuously talk to. So we're always speaking to the same people, and there's a whole load of people out there that don't even know we exist."

"I think one of the things that we could do is go to charities that work with specific groups, and either do presentations or invite them to come along to observe meetings," she continues. "The Association for Medical Charities is a member of this shared commitment that we've done, so we're hoping that through them, they will disseminate some advice to their membership groups, and then their membership groups could approach us and we could teach them a bit more about what the HRA does. For autistic people, I mean, I think they'd love it – just love the depth."

The HRA has also been surveying its research ethics committees and confidentiality advisory groups to ascertain "what they think of working" for the research watchdog. The information collected from that is now being used to develop a strategy for diversifying these groups.

"We're at the beginning, so we don't know how it's going to look, how it's going to actually happen," Molony-Oates concedes. "What we've done is we've recognized that we're not as diverse as the population we're serving – and that's not right – but we haven't worked out how to actually change it completely. We're at the start of that journey."

Our conversation then moves to the state of public involvement, and again, to what makes it valuable. "Over the last 20 years, it's definitely got loads better," she says, "but now, we're looking at the quality of that, rather than just, 'yes, I did it, I put an ad on Facebook and 16 people replied', or, 'I got people to check that the consent form was readable'. Now we want more depth, and that work is going to take time to really embed it properly."

Another long process, but Molony-Oates speaks positively about research's future. "I think COVID did a huge amount of damage, but it also opened people's eyes a lot," she says, "and people are now much, much, much more aware of research than they were in the past, and they're aware of the value of research, and they also want to know what's happening. They don't want to just hand it off to some agency that will deal with it; they actually want to know what's going on.

"They're also very concerned about public money [...] Where is it going?" she continues. "So I think we have an opportunity now where the public are actually really, really interested in research, where we can drive this change. We're at a moment in time where the population is no longer willing to sit back and let other people do it. They want to know what's happening and they're not willing to allow things to be done to them or *for* them any more.

"We have to nurture our NHS," the public involvement manager states. "We have to really look after it. We can't be pushing the staff to do research that isn't going to be ultimately extremely valuable. So we need to be really, really careful and really look after the money that we're spending and I think that the general public is on board with that."

The drive for change, Molony-Oates goes on to add, is now coming in all directions. "It's coming from the bottom up and the top down and I think, as a result, we should see significant change, I think in ten years, absolutely," she says. "We're hoping to transform research so that we don't do *less* research, but we do it better. Better quality, more involvement, and better outcomes. If something goes wrong, that we talk about it as well – that's really important. If the research doesn't actually find out what they thought it would, that that gets published, because then nobody else is going to waste time doing that thing.

"That's huge, because a lot of the time research that doesn't actually prove what they set out to prove doesn't go anywhere, and that's a real pity – that we get all this lost data. Then you end up five years down the line, someone goes, 'oh, let's do some research on that', and there's no evidence that it's been done before because nobody wrote it up. [...] That's a whole other section of what the Health Research Authority wants – that transparency. We want reports back a year on about what's happened. Has it gone well? Has it not gone well? What worked, what didn't work? What can we learn from this, because we can learn from everything we do," Molony-Oates concludes.

Essentially, then, there has to be an element of evaluation, and by extension, the results of such an analysis need to be communicated with a wider audience.

Kelsey Martin, executive vice president of funding body the Simons Foundation (the organization behind the aforementioned SPARK study), sets this out when I ask her about the necessary improvements required of grant organizations. "I think they need to communicate really well," she says. "[It] is being clear about how we communicate the findings of the research, I think. It's hard because you're always moving really fast, everybody's trying to get things done. [It's about] taking the time to say, 'here's what this study that was funded by the Simons Foundation found'."

Except Dr Martin also concedes there's a problem with the terminology being used by researchers. "It's very easy to use a shorthand and say we're studying autism, when really what we're studying is a very specific behaviour. It's just a feature of what it means to be a human being," she explains. "I think that by using that shorthand, we probably contribute to a misunderstanding of what is autism. I'm going to add something: that I don't think it's specific to autism research. I think it's in many fields, and in particular, in fields of studying brain diseases, where we don't necessarily have the right... almost vocabulary about what it is we're studying. I think it's incumbent on scientists, on funders, on publishers, to be really clear in their discussions of what they are studying.

"I think we're very sloppy with our language, and to me, it's ironic, because I think, as scientists, the whole goal is to be really clear and precise and there's been a difficulty in doing that," Dr Martin continues. "This is just part of the challenge of people who are trained as scientists – whether it's as a geneticist, whether it's as a systems neuroscientist and electrophysicist – they have a real depth of knowledge in their field. If you're a clinician and you're interacting with autistic children, you have a different understanding of what it means to be autistic, and they're almost two different cultures. They also have their own vocabulary, and it's very difficult to get them to really interact. Again, I think this is true across all of biomedical research right now – how do we get three communities together? The clinical provider community, the participant community [...] and the scientific community."

It's about collaboration, and that's something that the executive vice president says the Simons Foundation is working hard on. "We try to listen to a lot of different voices and have a very open mind about, one, what are the really critical scientific questions that need to be addressed, and, two, what are the new areas in science and new emerging opportunities that we can try to fund, so that they actually have an impact," says Dr Martin. "So we do a lot of convening of people and that feeds into our grant making, and then we take our grant making and we try to make sure that the data that's generated – in a responsible way, that protects everybody's privacy – is available for other researchers to try to amplify the impact of that research. I think there's a necessity to be really clear about what we're funding research on."

The Simons Foundation's process seems, in summary, straightforward enough. "When we get grants that come in, when we put out requests for applications, and we get responses to those applications or submissions, we look at those internally first, and we think about the relevance to autism, and then we do send them out for external review," explains Dr Martin, adding that there's an internal scientific team within the Simons Foundation Autism Research Initiative (SFARI), as well as cohorts within its Searchlight genes project and its SPARK study, which the organization can call upon. "So we have peer review, and we believe pretty deeply in peer review, so we make sure that there are people who understand a lot of the science, because we want to make sure that it's actually really rigorous, well controlled, that the results are going to be interpretable, that they're going to yield information that will be reproducible – so it also goes through that level of peer review."

Alongside Dr Martin, I also reached out to the Wellcome Trust, funders of the controversial Spectrum 10K project among other studies. Their press office took three weeks to provide a response to an interview request, in which they confirmed they would provide a written comment instead, showing a lack of urgency for dealing with correspondence from journalists.

"We support research that tries to expand knowledge of

life, health and wellbeing," a spokesperson finally told me in an emailed statement. "We're open to ideas from researchers across a range of fields and disciplines, including those who seek to improve our understanding of the many different experiences of health. Applications for funding are rigorously reviewed by expert committees with subject-specific knowledge and expertise, and before any research begins, applicants must ensure they have appropriate ethical approval in place.

"Working with a group of experts from around the world," they add, "we are beginning to develop a set of principles to help ensure the research we fund is designed and undertaken in a more inclusive way. This could include how topics and questions are chosen, to who participates in research and how they gain from new discoveries."

The US's National Institutes of Health (NIH) didn't provide an official for interview either, and directed me to specific sections of its website. One on the review process reads: "Reviewers will provide an overall impact score to reflect their assessment of the likelihood for the project to exert a sustained, powerful influence on the research field(s) involved, in consideration of the following review criteria, and additional review criteria (as applicable for the project proposed)."[4]

The aforementioned criteria concern a study's significance, investigator(s), innovation, approach and environment. The "inclusion of women, minorities, and children" is a criterion for consideration "as applicable".

The second stage of the NIH's review process relates to advisory councils or boards consisting of "scientists from the extramural research community and public representatives". In contacting the National Institute of Neurological Disorders and Stroke (NINDS), I was redirected to the National Institute of Mental Health (NIMH), which I'm told provides considerable

---

4   National Institutes of Health (2021).

support for autism research. This specific institute's advisory council is that of the National Advisory Mental Health Council (NAMHC), made up of professors, medical professionals and heads of certain health organizations.

The involvement of advocates instead comes in the form of the Interagency Autism Coordinating Committee (IACC). Also under the NIMH, the federal advisory committee "provides advice and recommendations to the Secretary of Health and Human Services regarding federal activities related to autism spectrum disorder".[5] It currently has three self-advocates on its committee – one of which is Dr Morénike Giwa Onaiwu, to whom we have already been introduced.

There's promising developments from the NIH's National Institute on Deafness and Other Communication Disorders (NIDCD), too. In July 2023, it published a "request for information" from members of the public to comment on its "research directions to support communication in minimally verbal/non-speaking people". It came two months after it published a "notice of special interest" inviting research applications focusing on this particular topic. Dr Kristina Johnson, a postdoctoral fellow at Boston Children's Hospital, told *Spectrum* the April 2023 notice will be "a catalyst for change".[6]

Alongside grant bodies, journal editors too place their trust in autism researchers. In explaining the "significant responsibility" her journal feels in upholding high-quality research and trust in the industry, editor-in-chief of SAGE's *Autism* Professor Sue Fletcher-Watson says: "It also probably rests on a relationship of trust with the submitting authors. So, for example, they will make a statement in papers that they went through an ethical review process and we don't double check that statement. We just assume that it's true."

---

5   Interagency Autism Coordinating Committee (n.d.).
6   Dattaro (2023).

Why is that? "I would say, resourcing and labour," she replies. "I don't know of any journals that check it. So, there is an assumption that people are being honest and truthful, and that fraudulent behaviour is in a tiny minority and would normally be picked up in other ways.

"I think if you have not bothered to get ethics for your research, there will probably be other indicators as well. There'll be reasons why we wouldn't want to publish it," Professor Fletcher-Watson continues. "So I think there is a responsibility there, but our responsibility does not replace the position of the researcher themselves, the institution where they're employed, the ethics committee and policies within that institution – all of those steps and processes that happened before a piece of finished work is submitted to the journal."

I mention these points to *Autism Research* journal editor Dr David Amaral, who brings up a recent conversation with his ophthalmologist son-in-law: "We were discussing over the weekend these new AI chat boxes that are available and are capable of writing a very credible paper. The papers that can come out right now are difficult to determine whether they were created by computer as opposed to a person, and I think that's going to get more and more sophisticated," he warns.

Then there's the fact the publication process is also dependent on several presumptions. "One is that the research that's carried out was carried out ethically and it was carried out with high standards. So obviously, you can't fabricate data and there's a number of rules that scientists learn as they get their PhD and medical degrees about how to do research," adds Dr Amaral. "So you start with the presumption that people are going to follow those rules and then in the review process, we try and ask experts in the area of a particular paper to evaluate whether they think the paper has [been done properly]."

Even incoming editors-in-chief are realizing the benefits of specialist editors. In a February 2023 editorial, Lynn Kern

Koegel of the *Journal of Autism and Developmental Disorders* (*JADD*) wrote: "Due to the large number of submissions, we are attempting to streamline the review process by adding a group of topic editors who will evaluate submissions based on topic, design, novelty, and contribution to decide whether they are suitable to go to peer review. We hope this process will save time for authors and reviewers."

Kern Koegel – who authored a book in 2014 called *Overcoming Autism*, of which the first chapter is titled "Diagnosis: Surviving the Worst News You'll Ever Get" – also confirmed the journal would be ditching its case history category, seeing as autism is "no longer a rare condition".

Though of course, whenever individuals are brought in to comment on autism research, soon comes the question of just how many autistic people get to weigh in on important decisions. In the case of journals, how do they ensure such a demographic gets a say in the type of studies they publish?

"Honestly, I don't think we do that in a formalized way," admits Professor Fletcher-Watson. "I think we actually do it a lot more than most other journals do, but it's all via informal routes. It's about the editors that we recruit, and the relationship that they have with the broader kind of autism community and autistic community specifically. We're looking for editors who share a sort of value system, and that value system that foregrounds autistic perspectives and wellbeing, and then that value system goes along with considering themselves part of this community of people who are invested in learning useful things about what it is like to be autistic, right?

"What we don't have, for example, is an autistic peer reviewer on every publication," she continues. "I know *Autism in Adulthood* does; I think it's incredibly admirable."

The editor-in-chief offers to explain why *Autism* does things differently, and I take her up on that. "I think two factors have led me to hesitate introducing this. One is really the sort of scale of the labour involved and the relatively small numbers of autistic academics," she explains. "I mean, peer review is already free labour, right? So there's already a problem with peer review. You're asking autistic academics – of whom there are a limited number, especially out autistic and non-autistic academics – to take on this extra burden of doing peer review. You're also looking for them to have specific expertise in the topic, so they're bringing, obviously, their lived experience, but they should also be knowledgeable about the topic.

"We include autistic reviewers, we have many autistic reviewers in our pool and of course we draw on them as far as we possibly can, but if we made a statement to include an autistic reviewer in every paper, and then we have 800 submissions a year submitted to our journal, I worry about the burden aspect of that," explains Professor Fletcher-Watson.

Dr Amaral points towards a similar problem. "I was thinking about this the other day, that we treat all people equally, we base our requests for advice on expertise, not whether you're white, Black, male, female, autistic or non-autistic," he says. "At least for the time being, we don't want to make the process a political process. It's not whether this might be pro autism. It's just like the language debate right now, right? It's more of a political issue than a scientific issue, and my job is to make sure that how we run the journal is based on evaluating papers for their scientific quality, not 'Are they pro neurodiversity? Are they perceived as being anti-neurodiversity?' (unless it's a paper on neurodiversity).

"For a scientific paper, that shouldn't be part of the value structure," stresses Dr Amaral. "It really is: was the paper done well [...]? So, we don't rule out autistic people from participating, but we rule them in just like we would rule anybody else in, based on their expertise."

He later goes on to add, "I would hesitate at the moment [...] to say we always have to have an autistic individual review [a study]. It's sort of like in the United States, there has been a time – I think it's changing now – where every committee had to have a Black individual on the committee, right? There'll be some university, some places where, because of the relatively smaller number of Black academics, they were being asked to be on every damn committee you can imagine, and it was really a burden on that segment of our community."

This doesn't mean *Autism Research* doesn't try to involve autistic people "more and more" in the journal's review process to the greatest extent possible. "We don't have a specific policy that a paper has to be reviewed by an autistic individual, but on the other hand, all of our associate editors are increasingly aware of who are the autistic scientists that they can rely on," stresses Dr Amaral. "For example, we had a series of papers on terminology to be used in *Autism Research* recently and we ensured that those papers which really did affect the autistic community, that we would have an autistic individual be at least one of the reviewers for those papers. So it's sort of a constant assessment of whether a paper has been done properly, whether it's believable, and it's based on trying to get experts in the field who have enough experience with the topic, that they can help us make those judgements."

Autism Research's reviewers are also made anonymous. "I think it would be harder for us to get reviewers if we lost the anonymity," admits Dr Amaral. "You can imagine a younger reviewer is not going to criticize necessarily a senior, well-known, powerful author to the extent that they would rightfully, if they could be anonymous. So we just decided to continue in that sort of old-fashioned policy of keeping the reviewers anonymous."

The journal is even considering extending the anonymity out to cover the study authors too, in a "double blind" approach. "Right now, the reviewers know the authors, so they know where the paper comes from, who the authors are," its editor continues. "Some have raised the issue, 'well, that sort of potentially leads to bias in the reviewers' minds'.

"We're considering it. I'm not sure if and when we'll make a decision about that. It's really hard to go double blind because you can imagine that you have to scrub the entire paper of anything that indicates where the research came from. So it's difficult for the authors and it's difficult for the journal to make sure that everything has been scrubbed."

Dr Amaral tells me he is yet to reach the conclusion that a double blind is "absolutely essential", but it would certainly serve as another way in which to remove bias and therefore political influence from a predominantly scientific and objective practice.

Meanwhile, Professor Fletcher-Watson is considering another issue. "One thing that we have as well is a community involvement statement, which is a compulsory part of the submission, though I will say we're currently evaluating that because it definitely has downsides as well as positives," she reveals to me. "I worry, personally, about autistic researchers in the field feeling compelled to out themselves in print in order to meet the expectations of the community statement. We have stated very clearly that the purpose of it is to capture formalized participatory methods, reaching out to autistic people who are not necessarily within academia. That's the function of that statement, to give a space to report those engagement methods and involvement methods, but I can see how an autistic researcher who has not done a formal external engagement, but is themselves autistic, might feel very uncomfortable to write, 'there was no community involvement in this study', right? Because they're like, 'well, I'm here'.

"So I think there's some tension there, and that's something that we're sort of working on at the journal to resolve – how do we encourage that engagement, without putting individual authors or researchers or contributors into a position where they need to share something that is confidential?"

How does one strike such a balance, I ask Professor Fletcher-Watson later on in our conversation – with the understanding, of course, that the work to unpack such a dilemma is ongoing. "We've given people some sample text that they can use that say things like, 'the leadership team for this research is neurodiverse', say, or other variations on that, essentially," she replies. "So something that doesn't name an individual or even name a particular diagnosis, in fact, and just sort of indicates that there was some involvement. The opposite strategy to that is to make it clear that the community involvement section is about formalized involvement and engagement methods.

"Maybe we need to sort of change the name of the piece, and call it 'participatory methods', and then you can say, 'we didn't use any participatory methods'. You don't have to say, 'no autistic people are involved in this research', you know?"

Perhaps unsurprisingly, Dr Amy Price of the *British Medical Journal (BMJ)* is a fan of the journal's own review process. "The *BMJ* has a team of editors that decides about every paper, so it's never one editor deciding whether a paper is published or it's not," she details. "It's a committee of really thoughtful clinicians, researchers, policymakers, statisticians, and they meet every week to decide on the papers that are going to be included that week. They read the paper themselves and then they look at the input from our peer reviewers and also from our public reviewers.

"Our public reviewers and our peer reviewers have equal weight," Dr Price continues, "so no one person makes any decision about a *BMJ* paper, and no one peer or public reviewer decides if it can be published or if it can't."

Much like the NIH, *The Lancet* – the journal which infamously published, and then retracted, Andrew Wakefield's damaging 1998 paper – decided to direct me to several webpages and the work of the *Lancet* Commission on "the future of care and clinical research in autism", rather than provide an expert for comment.

The information on its peer review process is pretty succinct.[7] "All research articles submitted to the *Lancet* journals are first reviewed by our in-house team of expert editors," the journal states. "A high proportion of research papers are rejected on the basis of in-house assessment alone. If editors wish to proceed with a paper, they will select appropriate peer reviewers.

"During peer review, editors select reviewers to reflect relevant expertise, diversity, and geographical backgrounds," the page continues. "All original research articles published in the *Lancet* journals have undergone independent, external peer review, including statistical review. A research article is usually peer reviewed by three clinical or subject-based experts and a statistical reviewer."

While the *Lancet* Commission's 2022 paper looks more at care and support for autistic people – arguing for a "stepped care and personalised health approach" when it comes to autism – it too examines and critiques autism research, arguing, "the gap between what [it] currently offers" and the needs of autistic individuals and communities "calls for action and rethinking of the science of clinical practice in this field".[8] The Commission's most compelling arguments are simply commonsense recommendations. For instance, in pushing for a move "beyond single investigator-led (albeit multisite) studies to more integrated attempts that take into account individual differences within autism", the Commission is evidently – to put it in far simpler terms – calling for greater recognition of neurodiversity within the industry. It isn't the only body to make this point.

7   *The Lancet* (2023).

8   Lord et al. (2022).

"Recognition of human diversity helps us to better understand autistic individuals in ways that have far-reaching effects," the report reads. "These effects cut across issues as broad as human rights, equity and social justice, respect for difference, and the need to take individual and family preferences into account. Valuing neurodiversity has the potential to create stronger and wiser communities and positive social values."

Acknowledging autism's existence beyond childhood and meaningful consultation with autistic people are also highlighted by the Commission. "Research on autism in adulthood in general is scarce and relatively recent [...] that on older adults is almost non-existent, and a pressing need exists for funding agencies and researchers to prioritise intervention and evaluation research across the whole ability range and lifespan," it states. "In addition, the inclusion of people with lived experience of autism in the planning of and doing such research is increasingly recognised as essential."

Yet it also proposes the adoption of "profound autism" to denote "individuals who are very likely to need substantial support throughout their lives, but still have opportunities for improved quality of life through positive daily activities, supported independence in everyday actions, and social contacts".

As mentioned previously, the term is controversial, with "high support needs" preferred by many autistic people as an alternative. An open letter to the Commission in February 2022, signed by international organizations representing autistic people such as ASAN, the European Council of Autistic People and the Autistic Collaboration Trust, labelled such a proposal as "highly problematic". It also claimed participatory research was "mentioned but not defined".[9]

In comments published by *Spectrum* in the same year, co-chairs Tony Charman and Catherine Lord stressed the label was

---

9   Autistic Self Advocacy Network (2022).

not "mandatory", but rather to denote and "highlight" autistic children and adults in need of lifelong support and with higher support needs.

Areas of contention are brought up by Dr Amy Price of the *BMJ*, too, who says candidly: "There's so much bitterness behind whatever has happened to people that often they can't let go of that. So there's giving them space and finding a place to be understanding.

"The thing is, even when you've been treated badly, and you have every right to retaliate and to be hostile, when you do that, there's no place to stop, so your enemies can never be quite dead enough," Dr Price continues. "Even if you don't have equity and you take the high road, then other people slowly start to follow that example. Some people never will, but then they exclude themselves."

As a brief aside, Dr Dave Caudel of Vanderbilt University cites a similar example from personal experience during our conversation, specifically in relation to ABA. "Misunderstandings can frequently come about because we're both using the same words, but they might have very different connotations," he explains. "What is referred to as ABA today – when it's properly applied in certain circumstances – is absolutely beneficial, and we shouldn't throw out the baby with the bathwater. Now, when I'm talking to the ABA specialists and such I'm like, 'you need to be aware of this history and you need to be aware of this pain and this trauma, and if you ever get an autistic person coming at you with a lot of rage and such, you need to understand where that's coming from and we need to deal with that with compassion and understanding'.

"I have seen conversations where somebody is staunchly opposed to ABA," the researcher continues. "It's really hard to have a conversation with them, because they're just so emotional about it. The researchers listened to them and their perspective and talked about their perspective and had that dialogue.

I'm not going to say that that person is an ABA advocate now, but I think that person did concede, 'OK, yeah, in certain contexts, with the right people, I can see where potentially that does have some benefit.' You could see there was an understanding and a bit more of a shared perspective.

"It's not simple and it's not trivial, there's not an easy answer to that," acknowledges Dr Caudel. "It all starts with sympathy and I would go one step further and say empathy. It all starts with being empathetic and recognizing this is why this population is so fired up about it."

Dr Price's comments obviously transcend specific, targeted improvements for autism research journals. On that issue, Professor Fletcher-Watson's response is frank. "My first thought is to stop publishing really awful research, but then, it's really glib, isn't it?" she says. "Because the whole point is who gets to define what's awful or not? Even stuff that has negative elements can have a sort of kernel of something valuable in it.

"I often think of doing research as like sort of adding a grain of sand to a beach," continues Professor Fletcher-Watson. "It's just tiny, tiny, tiny, but the whole beach of research-based knowledge about autism – I think, broadly – is helping, parts of it are helping. Even the theory of mind and the empathy [hypothesis]... Would we have the double empathy problem if we hadn't first had the empathizing quotient?"

The pushback against the negative papers, she explains, inspires some of the more positive research – and it's the good-quality work that the researcher says the journal needs to uplift more.

"I think we could probably do more to showcase and promote the things that we think have really done a great job across the board. Excellent methods, excellent analysis, excellent engagement with community priorities," she concedes. "It's not an either/or choice, you can do all of these things, and when we find those examples that we think are really good, we should be boosting them.

"I think we could do more to be more transparent about our processes, so that people at least understand what's going on behind the scenes," the professor adds. "Apart from anything else, it's hard to critique a structure that you can't see or understand." She also talks about making the journal's work more accessible. "We have lay abstracts in our journal, but someone's just actually submitted a paper which we're going to publish, which is an analysis of the readability of the lay abstracts in our journal. It's like, 'they're not really readable enough'. They're better than the regular scientific abstracts, but they're not as readable as you ideally want to make them, to make them really accessible to people."

The accessibility of abstracts is also brought up by Dr Amaral: "Several years ago, we included a lay abstract for all our articles in the journal, because many of the autism community members, families and others probably don't have the background to be able to read the content, knowledgeably, of the paper. We want to make sure at least they get the bottom line of each of the papers that are being published," he explains. "So we started that a few years back and we've now had some feedback that – I think this is true – we haven't been rigorous enough in setting standards for the lay abstracts, meaning that they're still too complicated.

"Authors would often take their big abstract – their scientific abstract – and just take out a few words and turn it into the lay abstract. But really, we wanted to get maybe the way you [Liam] would write, or a structure that virtually anybody could understand and understand the take-home message."

Dr Price is already thinking of other ways in which a paper's findings can be communicated. "One of the challenges that we have is that the systems that the papers are built in – the journal systems – are seriously outmoded," she explains. "It would be wonderful to be able to run video journal articles. So maybe a five-minute video and that's actually a part of the article, or to upload actual working code so that you could execute it right within the paper, things like that."

Opening up the freedom of choice around how the autistic community can receive details of a paper is essential to ensuring as many autistic people can access research as possible. Empowering the autistic community should be at the centre of all autism research, and accessibility – and the independence that can bring – is a huge part of that.

So too are our politicians, and the empowerment they can secure for autistic people through new rights in legislation – politicians who can also be influenced by autism researchers and the industry's overarching narrative.

Chapter 10

POLITICAL PERSUASION

I was feeling out of place, in a suit, in the middle of Trafalgar Square on a spring afternoon. It was March 2022, and against a flood of colour from Deaf people around me – an ever-expressive community, complete with vibrant placards and an impressive sense of style – I stood ready to present a TV news package in an unremarkable, monochrome outfit.

The event itself was a rally in support of a British Sign Language (BSL) bill, which was having its third and final reading in the House of Commons that afternoon – exactly 19 years to the day that the UK formally recognized BSL in the chamber. The draft legislation, put forward by former Labour MP Rosie Cooper, looked to extend that further, by recognizing BSL in law.

I mention this here not only out of an obvious, personal love for Deaf culture, but because it was a landmark piece of legislation, placing a fresh description of a community of marginalized people on the statute book.

Whether it's an accurate description, or indeed a meaningful contribution to law, continues to be fiercely contested – given its limitations to Great Britain as opposed to the UK, and it granting no new legal rights to Deaf BSL citizens.

Autism's version of such significant legislation in the UK came, arguably, in the form of the Autism Act 2009. First introduced by the late Conservative MP Dame Cheryl Gillan, and sponsored by Labour peer Baroness Jill Pitkeathley, it concerns "meeting the needs of adults with autistic spectrum conditions; and for connected purposes".

More specifically, it called on the UK government to develop an autism strategy for England and issue guidance to support it. The first iteration of such a strategy, *Fulfilling and Rewarding Lives*, came a year later.[1]

"[Our vision is that] all adults with autism are able to live fulfilling and rewarding lives within a society that accepts and understands them," the first section begins. "They can get a diagnosis and access support if they need it, and they can depend on mainstream public services to treat them fairly as individuals, helping them make the most of their talents."

Rather helpfully, the strategy can be condensed down into its five key areas: "increasing awareness and understanding" among frontline professionals; producing a clear and consistent diagnostic pathway followed by "the offer of a personalised needs assessment"; improving access to services which support autistic adults to live independently within the community; employment; and the development of local services.

By 2021, the strategy had expanded to include autistic children and young people.[2] Health and care inequalities, inpatient care and support within the criminal justice system had specific sections in the policy – sections which drew upon autism research.

This is to be expected, of course. We trust our politicians to pass policy that enhances the quality of life for the electorate, based on research that encapsulates and draws upon their lived experiences. Their relationship is symbiotic; the need to have trust in both parties is essential.

---

1   Department of Health (2010).
2   Department of Health and Social Care (2021).

"I think research influenced it, but in my view – and you would expect me to say this because I'm a campaigner, that's what I do – the lobby is always as much [an] influence as the research," says Baroness Pitkeathley, the peer who saw the Autism Act through its final stages in the Lords. "I think the lobby probably starts it. It begins with a lobby; begins with users; with carers, in my case; with victims; with sufferers; however you want to put that.

"The research then comes in on the back of that, to back it up, but I think the research is the secondary thing," she continues. "The groundswell of lobbying and opinion is first, but you would expect me to say that because I'm a campaigner, not a researcher."

It makes sense. Politicians like to learn about the people; the individuals who leap out of the research briefings and share experiences that are difficult to confine to numbers and statistics – figures that can be so easily brushed aside by decision-makers.

"Statistics and facts are always open to different interpretations," says Baroness Pitkeathley, in remarks not too far removed from my own about the collapse of a universal truth – outlined in this book's introduction. "Yesterday [21 January 2023] we had a minister giving statistics about the number of [asylum-seeking] children who've gone missing from hotels, and the statistics they quoted were totally different from the ones the questioners were quoting. So you've always got to bear in mind there may be a political slant to how you quote statistics."

Jessica Benham, an autistic legislator in Pennsylvania's House of Representatives, warns of a similar issue. "It's important for policymakers to be aware that it is easy for non-experts to misinterpret or misuse research," she writes over email, acknowledging there are "many areas where I am not an expert" and subject to "the same potential pitfalls". Representative Benham adds that she often prefers to speak and ask questions of researchers, in addition to reading the research itself.

In asking Baroness Pitkeathley how she sees the relationship between researchers and policymakers, she too speaks of documentation. "If I'm doing a speech, I hope that I will get a briefing. If I put a question down, I will hope to get a briefing," the Lords member explains. "I think the difficulty is, that research [and] academia don't quite always get the politics. They don't quite always get [that] it takes a very long time to change policy, it's very difficult to change policy, and you can't get what you want. It's always got to be a compromise."

A concept with which autism researchers, if carrying out their studies correctly, will already be familiar – through the process of meaningful consultation. In fact, it's the involvement of members of the community in question that often grabs the attention of policymakers.

"Policymakers should engage with research," says Representative Benham, "but should also listen to people with lived experience."

Baroness Pitkeathley goes further in her suggested improvements to research. "[Be] swift, quick, don't take years over it, and always root it in that user experience," she tells me, "and that's what makes it authentic, I would say, and that's what policymakers like."

Up until this point in the book, both numerous contributors and I have made the case that autism researchers and academia establish a narrative around the condition, which is critiqued by autistic advocates, adopted by charitable organizations and supported by ethics boards and journals. Politicians play their part through passing policy and legislation informed by such research, enshrining the narrative in the statute books and mandating action that shapes the lives of autistic people in one way or another.

Baroness Pitkeathley, however, has a different view. "I don't think the research sets the narrative; I think the lobby set the narrative," she argues, "so I don't agree with that statement."

Except "the lobby" in this case, made up of campaign groups, charities and activists, will all obtain their facts and figures about autism from the same source material: academia. Whether it's in the background or at the forefront of influencing elected representatives, research leaves a mark in political discourse – therefore it must always be substantiated and robust.

"I certainly feel a huge responsibility to the lobby, to the users – that is my principal driver and it's something I'm constantly saying," the policymaker continues.

Of course, having autistic people with their own lived experience sitting in the halls of democracy would be the most ideal scenario, in the interests of first-hand advocacy, but at the time of writing, there are only a few high-profile examples.

The ex-Sheffield Hallam MP Jared O'Mara – whose time as the constituency's representative was marred by previous homophobic and sexist comments, a staff resignation via the MP's own Twitter account, and a conviction for fraud – considered himself the first autistic member of parliament to sit in the UK House of Commons. He only served for two years, however, deciding to step down when the 2019 general election came around.

Across the pond, there's been some success at state level. Joining Representative Benham are Texas representative Briscoe Cain, and former New York state assembly member Yuh-Line Niou – the latter of which lost a contest to represent her state in Congress at the end of 2022, which would have made her the first openly autistic member if she was successful in her campaign.

Such a bid nevertheless stands in stark contrast to the attitudes towards autism held in the US more than 15 years prior. The Combating Autism Act of 2006 amended the Public Health Service Act to "combat autism through research, screening, intervention and education". The full text of the Act goes one further, to talk of expanded research from the National Institutes of Health which investigates "the cause [...] diagnosis or rule out, early detection, prevention, services, supports, intervention, and treatment of autism spectrum disorder".

The language of the Act was clearly concerning, in its talk of "prevention" and painting autism as a "disorder", rather than a condition. President George W. Bush's remarks upon signing it into law further demonstrated the troubling discourse at the time.[3]

"For millions of Americans whose lives are affected by autism," he said, "today is a day of hope. The Combating Autism Act of 2006 will increase public awareness about this disorder and provide enhanced federal support for autism research and treatment.

"By creating a national education program for doctors and the public about autism, this legislation will help more people recognize the symptoms of autism," Bush continued. "This will lead to early identification and intervention, which is critical for children with autism. I am proud to sign this bill into law and confident that it will serve as an important foundation for our nation's efforts to find a cure for autism."

The aggressive terminology was taken to another level by Jon Shestack, co-founder of Cure Autism Now (the parent-led non-profit which later merged with Autism Speaks), who reportedly described the Act as "a federal declaration of war on the epidemic of autism".[4]

Referencing Shestack's comments a year later, Ari Ne'eman, then president of ASAN, said the narrative of a "war on autism" was "not in the interests of people on the spectrum".[5]

"It offends and alienates the autistic community," he said. "This is the community of verbal and nonverbal individuals on

3   Bush (2006).

4   O'Keefe (2006).

5   Autism Self Advocacy Network (2007).

the autism spectrum – distinguishable from the autism community of the parents, professionals and others who often claim to speak on our behalf.

"We are usually the last to be consulted on autism policy," he went on to add. "The autistic community should be the first to have input into policymaking about our own futures."

Not to mention that this legislation falls into the trap of painting autism as a condition that only occurs in childhood. In 2016, a decade on from the Act, Californian professor and author of *The Politics of Autism*, John J. Pitney Jr, said in a speech to the Richard Nixon Foundation: "If you hear politicians talk about [autism], they'll almost always talk about it in the context of kids with autism [...] but children with autism become adults with autism.

"This is something that politicians aren't talking about," he continues, "so if ever you get a chance to talk to elected officials, ask them about autistic adults. What are we doing for adults on the spectrum, to help them adjust to society? The more they hear from people about this question, the more they might start thinking more seriously about it."

In contrast to the UK, where additional legislation over time expanded policies to cover autistic *children* as well as adults, the US found itself finally acknowledging autism in adulthood in the form of the Autism Collaboration, Accountability, Research, Education and Support Act of 2019 – or the Autism CARES Act for short.

Alongside renewing funding until 2024, the official website of the US Congress summarizes it as an Act that also "revises the scope" of programmes and activities to "encompass [autistic] individuals of all ages, rather than only youth", with "individuals" being the term the bill opts for instead of "children" from previous versions. Widening autism as an identity, and understanding it as one that isn't unique to children, makes it much harder for policymakers to view autistic people as monolithic – a perception that has plagued politicians as much as it has the world of academia.

Fortunately, even beyond the realms of legislation itself, there are other ways in which campaigners, charities and other lobbyists can influence the political discourse around autism. More specifically, the UK's democratic system allows for a more informal method of drawing politicians' attention to the needs of autistic people. All-Party Parliamentary Groups – or APPGs – are not official parliamentary bodies in the way select committees are, but unite policymakers of any party under a particular topic or area of interest. According to statistics contained in a report by the House of Commons Committee on Standards in April 2022, more than 750 APPGs were registered in February of that year. Subjects ranged from "jazz appreciation" to "pigeon racing".[6]

There is, of course, one for autism, set up to "raise awareness of issues affecting autistic people, their families and carers; to raise parliamentary awareness of autism; to campaign for changes to government policy to benefit autistic people and improve diagnosis or support for autistic people". It's supported by NAS as its secretariat, and an advisory group currently made up of autistic advocates, researchers, medical professionals, charities and non-profits.

Meanwhile, in America, there's a powerful lobby surrounding the often-harmful practice that is ABA. Autism Speaks – which listed spending of $53.5 million towards "understanding and acceptance" in the 2022 financial year[7] – has long expressed its support for the "treatment", and in February of that year wrote that "after years of advocacy by Autism Speaks", ABA was now a "covered benefit for Medicaid enrolees in Texas".[8]

---

6   House of Commons' Committee on Standards (2022).

7   Autism Speaks (2022a).

8   Autism Speaks (2022b).

Other news articles on its website hail steps to increase access to ABA in states such as Oklahoma and New York. It's hardly surprising that autistic activists hold Autism Speaks in such contempt, when the organization's spending on "understanding and acceptance" (which likely includes its advocacy work) in 2022 is almost three times as much as its spending on "services and support" ($15.7 million).

Of course, there's no denying that autism is, in itself, political. It's the first sentence in Professor Pitney Jr's *The Politics of Autism*, and one he expands upon by saying, "just about everything concerning autism is subject to dispute".

Though there is, of course, another institution that can prove itself to be just as provocative and incendiary when it comes to the ongoing discourse around autistic people, capable of stirring up moral panics and amplifying any research or study it considers noteworthy – and that's the media.

Chapter 11

PRESSING MATTERS

I am a small minority in my own industry. In the UK, the 2023 *Diversity in Journalism* report commissioned by the National Council for the Training of Journalists (NCTJ) found that, based on the latest Labour Force Survey data, just 22% of all journalists have a "work-limiting health condition or disability".[1]

This is a steady increase from 2018 and 2020 (which were 15% and 16% respectively), but it could and should always be higher. According to the Department for Work and Pensions' Family Resources Survey for the 2022–23 financial year, 24% of people in the UK were disabled.[2]

A quick look at the first handful of news articles that appear after a search online for "autism" makes clear the effect this lack of lived experience has on reporting. I've seen many pieces that mention "people with autism", despite many autistic people preferring to be called just that: autistic people.

The value in getting these things right in the journalism industry cannot be overstated. There is, obviously, the essential principle of accuracy, but there's also the important ideals of authenticity and reality. Just as much as researchers need to truly

---

1   Spilsbury (2023).
2   Department for Work and Pensions (2024).

listen to autistic people, journalists must do the same. They must not assume language preferences, or give in to the sensationalism that still surrounds so much of disability discourse.

I think back to the media's contribution to the moral panic over MMR – with its false, alarmist headlines – and, more recently, Spectrum 10K, as two examples. In terms of the latter, news organizations fawned over a number of high-profile celebrity ambassadors backing the Cambridge research project, instead of scrutinizing the actual science and ethics associated with it, or listening to the wider autistic community's concerns.

I published my first report on Spectrum 10K in August 2021 – when the study was first announced – for *indy100*. Titled 'What is the Spectrum 10K DNA study into autism – and why are autistic people concerned?', the piece mentioned the endorsements from public figures (for both balance and context, naturally), but leant more heavily into the wide range of legitimate concerns raised by autistic advocates. The article received widespread praise online, from members of a community who weren't used to a mainstream media outlet listening so intently to the issues they had raised.

It was lovely feedback to receive, but it was also damning of the industry. It's a serious problem when those tasked with amplifying research studies of significant public interest, and contributing to the narratives surrounding them, are met with disdain from marginalized communities. Why?

"I think one of the things the news media has done that, I would go as far as to say, has increased mistrust or decreased trust in all areas of human life – but certainly in science and, therefore, in autism research – is just every story has to be too definitive, right?" says Ivan Oransky, editor-in-chief of the autism research news outlet *Spectrum*. "'Oh, well, no, I'm not gonna click on that if you say that "here's something we know, and we don't know these other things".'"

It's sort of like a whiplash, he goes on to explain. "You had that with everything during the pandemic, whether it's vaccines, whether it's masks, and the fact that something changed a little bit," he says, "because we learned more, meant that people were accusing science of 'flip-flopping' and couldn't trust any of it.

"I think this has been playing out in many ways, over time, in many fields – including autism research," Oransky continues. "I think that that has made people weary and maybe even mistrustful of what they're reading and then, therefore, of the science itself. Like, 'make up your minds'. Well, no, science isn't about making up your minds; science is actually about learning more, right? So I think that journalism is complicit in that.

He adds: "I don't know that it's necessarily about the relationship that journalists have with autism research – although I would like to think about that, and that might actually also contribute – but I think it's more fundamentally about the way that science is covered as if it's a football match and someone wins each time, and that's not what it is."

Multidisciplinary storyteller Dev Ramsawakh details another absolute. "I've worked with different news organizations and there's a resistance to actually understanding disability and seeing it from a holistic, very human perspective and not just like, 'oh, this is a sad, tragic thing that's happening to other people and we should feel bad for them because they have this sad, tragic thing'," they explain, arguing that the news plays a "big part" in research being "stuck" in a care and medical model approach.

"[They] have really contributed to that idea of 'we're tragic', and then also just in terms who gets to be autistic," he continues. "The news is very focused on white, cisgender, otherwise able-bodied, middle-class to upper-class, especially male representation.

"I think gender, race, class, all of those things play into who is allowed to act in certain ways, who's allowed to express certain traits, and who is given that sort of leeway of, 'oh, you have this diagnosis, so that means we're going to let it slide, we know that's a thing because of that'," adds Ramsawakh.

Spectrum, I learn, is more specific in its focus when covering certain demographics. "A lot of what we're covering is not in humans," Oransky tells me, "but in terms of human studies, we try our best to be very explicit about what the population was – if they only looked at a certain population, maybe [a] certain socioeconomic or demographic group, or people with particular behavioural characteristics that are not shared by everyone, or vice versa."

This is just one editorial procedure followed by the news outlet, with another process in place when it comes to what studies they choose to cover. "First, we are thinking about, well, is this a well-done study? Are the findings interesting? Does it tell us something new about the field, about the basic science of autism?" explains Oransky. "So for that, we look for studies, and then in many cases, we send them out to an expert – so an expert in that particular subfield. Now that could be someone we've talked to before, it could be somebody whose work is cited in that research. We have a whole process for that and we discuss their responses as a group."

Spectrum also has an editorial advisory board, available to provide advice on a range of issues arising from the outlet's work.

"To be perfectly honest, we're still – and I think a lot of people are – grappling with what it means to cover a field where sometimes the research is not done with everyone's interests in mind, and what does that mean," admits Oransky. "Do we ignore that research? I actually think that pretending it doesn't exist doesn't really help anyone, right? So, not covering it at all just because of that would be problematic.

"How do we get to the bigger existential questions that people are asking, on every side of this and from every perspective, about what kind of research should be done? What kind of research is helpful?" he continues. "I hate the term 'chilling effect', but what we would hope is that what comes out of it is better research and more useful research that actually tells us something, as opposed to shutting down certain lines of enquiry. Rather than shutting down, is there a way to do them better? Is there a way to, again, lift everyone up?"

It's a dilemma that has reared its head before, not least when it came to the UK's referendum in 2016 on whether to leave the European Union. The "Vote Leave" campaign would repeatedly claim the country sent £350 million a week to the EU which could be better spent on the NHS – even though statisticians pointed out that former Prime Minister Margaret Thatcher had negotiated a "rebate" or discount on that weekly fee. The sum *actually* sent to the bloc was much less.

The challenge was calling it out, as the news industry's focus on balance meant a requirement to highlight both campaigns, even when one was constantly peddling a falsehood. To fact-check the argument was to platform harmful inaccuracies, but to ignore it would be to allow it to spread unchallenged, and to prompt accusations of bias.

This is politics, but it appears some autism researchers possess a dislike towards interrogation and examination as well. It's been explored in prior chapters, but Oransky's noticed it too.

"They're not monolithic, but one trend we've certainly seen is that because their work comes under scrutiny when it's covered, they sometimes are more wary. They are maybe a bit more distrustful," he tells me. "I mean, in other words, if you're studying astrophysics, and you've discovered a new planet, there's not a lot of tension around that. I know there is, in the scientific community – maybe Pluto, okay, fine – but that isn't on the same existential level as when you're studying a condition, for lack of a better term, or studying a phenomenon that people have very strong feelings about."

There's the absolutism of the news media, and the desire of

autism researchers to protect their legacy – and Oransky be-lieves the two are related.

"They're sort of born of the same parent, right?" he suggests. "Again, this I see in my work with [specialist outlet] Retraction Watch more than anything else, so admitting errors might be admitting misconduct or fraud. I'm not condoning it, but you can sort of understand why people aren't going to do that, but sometimes they're not willing to admit just honest error, be-cause they think that they don't get the next grant, they don't get the next promotion and get whatever, but I think they're all related, right?"

The journalist brings up the cosmology analogy again. "Like, 'OK, I got it wrong, Pluto is a planet, or whatever'. OK, that's about your legacy, but it's not about you as a human being," he continues. "The problem for a lot of scientists is they can't separate those. In other words, when someone comes to you and says, 'you're doing something hurtful, you're doing hurtful research', and I don't want to read anyone's mind, but I'm will-ing to bet that some of the people going to people and saying that, they're deliberately not saying, 'you're a hurtful person, you're evil'.

"Some may be, that's its own thing, but I think a lot of people are legitimately saying, 'please, we'd like you to understand our perspective', and 'this is how it comes out', or 'this is what it looks like'.

"Sometimes the language is quite heated, but more impor-tantly, because researchers – like many of us – their identity is all about their work, rather than about their career and everything else," Oransky explains. "The minute you start to sort of say, 'that's problematic', then it's like, 'Oh my God, this could all go away.' We humans – including myself, clearly – are not good at existential, right? We don't do that well, for maybe obvious rea-sons, and when things feel existential, people don't react well.

I'm not defending them or anything else, it's just reality. I think that that gets back to some of it, too, you can't allow for nuance."

The direction in which autism research is heading also sparks tension, he adds. "So that does play out in [their] relationship to the media because some may be less willing to speak to people," Oransky says. "It's almost as if they start at a place where you have to earn their trust, in both directions, and that's interesting."

I ask him how he sees the relationship between the media and autism researchers working. "I think, generally speaking, researchers tend to believe that journalism is important and that media is important – some of that is just globally, not just about the research," he replies, "but for some of them, part of that is getting the word out about their work."

He brings up altmetrics – that is, the 'alternative metrics' used to measure reaction to academic research, such as tweets or mentions of the study or researcher in the media. These stats, Oransky says, often have an impact on a project's funding.

"I would say that those who are maybe a bit more seasoned or media savvy see that there's a sort of relationship you can build with the media that is one of mutual trust," he continues. "Some, either because they're not as seasoned or because they think about things differently, may look at the media as just purely a megaphone for them, and they'll want to do things like read your story before you publish it and sort of give you very specific critiques of it. They don't necessarily understand or respect the independence of the media."

I'm yet to encounter such pedantic behaviour from autism researchers myself, but past encounters have been close. Recorded interviews face-to-face or in-person are swapped for written responses over email; requests for comments with tight turnarounds – such is the fast-moving nature of journalism – are criticized in favour of allowing several working days for a response.

I can imagine Oransky coming across a few in his established career. While *Spectrum* is his current outlet of choice, he's taken on editorial positions at Medscape, MedPage Today and *Scientific American*. He's also the founder of the aforementioned blog Retraction Watch, the purpose of which is pretty self-explanatory.

Though it's his time at news agency Reuters Health, between 2009 and 2013, that he draws upon when I ask him about the fast-paced nature of news and what it means for the more detailed investigations spanning weeks or months, as opposed to a couple of hours on shift.

It was a question inspired by remarks from a journalist who opted not to include their comments in this book, but I feel it speaks to every reporter. Shift work at mainstream news outlets involves working on stories as and when they arise, while lengthier, detailed investigations are relegated to articles to pursue in our own time or when we (rarely) get a moment spare. Freedom comes when you're a freelance journalist – the limitations of contracted hours no longer apply, and you can dedicate far more time to a series exploring an issue far beyond the constraints of a single article.

Curiously, Oransky notes a "doubling down" from the larger, established outlets on the more extensive reports. "Also newer outlets that are exclusively about those, so I'm thinking of the Marshall Project, this is here in the States about incarceration in the prison system/criminal justice system.

"I still think there's always a place for breaking news," he continues. "So I'm a big fan of beat reporting. You actually have to do a lot of the daily stories and the hourly stories in order to get to the big stories, to understand them and also to develop sources. So I actually think that in a perfect world, they all work together."

Anyway, about Reuters Health. "When I started there, I realized that my team – the staff writers – were writing five, sometimes only four, but four or five items a day," explains Oransky.

"And I went, 'wait, this is about like, complex studies and clinical medicine and all kinds of things. Wait a second, we got to do something.' So I actually limited that to two a day, which is still tough, I want to be clear, but two a day is not four or five a day, right? You can breathe a little bit. It's still pretty rapid pace.

"Then at one point, I actually figured out a way, because I had this great reporter who already clearly had a big scoop in India, to go to India for two months, and his colleagues filled in and we got more freelancers and whatever else," he continues. "So I've always been a big believer in that and the way that he got those stories was by being a beat reporter who was doing two a day and other things. So, I think there's a way to sort of square that circle, but the economics have to work and that remains a challenge, and if anything, it's going to be a bigger challenge."

He concludes by drawing upon the move to non-profit journalism – be it an outlet like *Spectrum*, which is an editorially independent part of a wider non-profit organization, or outlets like the Marshall Project or ProPublica where it is a central part of what they do. Both models, he says, seem to be allowing for richer work.

Recent research papers examining a significant body of news reporting over time, meanwhile, have indicated shifts in the narrative put forward by mainstream news publications, but not always in ways that are completely positive. Academics Noa Lewin and Nameera Akhtar from the University of California, Santa Cruz (UCSC), reviewed 315 articles from the *Washington Post*, dated between 2007 and 2017, in their paper published in May 2020. One of several "points of interest" detailed in its abstract was that "later articles about autism were more likely to use words like 'neurodiversity', more likely to highlight strengths of autistic people, and more frequently described accommodations for autistic people", with a lesser focus on "identifying [the] causes of autism". A news report from UCSC summarizing the study, however, noted a continued appearance of the divisive "high-functioning" and "low-functioning" labels.[3]

Meanwhile in the UK, Karaminis et al. from Edge Hill University in Lancashire analysed articles about autism and/or autistic people in ten British newspapers from 2011 to 2020. The study – also published in 2022 – found the papers "emphasised the adversities associated with autism", stories had a "strong focus on children and boys rather than adults and girls", and there were "repeated references" to public figures and fictional characters in articles discussing the condition. Clearly, the picture painted of autism by the media could certainly be more expansive.

As much as his wide-ranging journalistic career gives Oransky a good sense of past and present journalistic practice – both generally, and in relation to autism research – his role as a distinguished writer in residence at New York University (NYU) offers him a solid insight into its future. "My students at NYU and a lot of journalists who are sort of starting out and really up-and-coming are really focused on solutions journalism," he explains. "So they're not actually as interested as we olds are in 'find all the problems'. They're like, 'No, no, no, you've been doing that, and we got to move forward.'"

The Solutions Journalism Network (SJN), who advocate for this specific style of reporting, provides a helpful definition of the phrase: "[It] investigates and explains, in a critical and clear-eyed way, how people try to solve widely shared problems. While journalists usually define news as 'what's gone wrong', solutions journalism tries to expand that definition: responses to problems are also newsworthy."[4]

It goes further than just pointing out the issue, and can point at best practice elsewhere and ask why they aren't doing

3   McNulty (2020).
4   Solutions Journalism Network (2023).

something similar. It decimates the throwaway response the SJN highlight, which is that the body or organization under fire is simply "doing the best we can" – not when another country is doing it better, they're not.

In a sense, I can't help but wonder if this book falls under this definition, too, as it goes beyond simply stating autism research has a problem with trust, and seeks to find solutions. If there's one main takeaway which has been established in interviews with contributors, it's that many know of the lack of trust in the industry; the challenge is how to address that. According to Oransky, there's room in reporting for both pointing out the problem, and highlighting ways to move forward.

"I think that journalists, particularly nowadays, need to think about their work as a conversation, and as a place that people are having conversations," he adds. "It's not about telling you the story and what that is. There's a role for that, because there is some aspect of being able to go places and see things that other people can't, but that's more with something like war reporting, or a similar beat.

"Being a witness is a critical part of journalism," states Oransky, "but there's also a part of it that is how do we convene conversations and let them flow and be a place where people have them and learn from that and then develop bigger stories from that?"

The discussions must be healthy and productive, of course. The desire of certain mainstream outlets to strike up discourse in the past so easily fell into sensationalism or medicalization, fuelling moral panics and amplifying falsehoods about autism which have seeped into the public consciousness.

It's perhaps unsurprising, then, that in terms of improvements to be made to reporting, Oransky calls for a move away from the "always misleading" single studies. Despite what the name may suggest, these quantitative, data-led projects focus on the behaviour of more than one individual – typically a small group of people. Though of course, such a tiny dataset is hardly enough to draw elaborate conclusions or any correlations. If the media is to extrapolate research outwards into the wider, philosophical questions and problems in order to generate a discussion, the prevalence of such findings must be scrutinized.

"I would love to see a lot of journalists get away from the single study syndrome," explains Oransky. "I understand why it happens, and in fact we do it at *Spectrum*, but the more we can get away from that, the better – or at least provide a lot of context when we do write about single studies."

I remember what I was taught when I was a journalism student. Alongside the 5Ws to establish when considering a story (who, what, where, when, how), the 'so what' question determined its newsworthiness, its wider significance and its impact.

If we journalists are to move towards a more proactive, problem-solving approach to research, one that seeks to understand the wider consequences of a study, then I can't help but wonder if the 'so what' of 'Journalism 101' should now move to 'now what', to serve the progressive, fast-moving nature of our work.

'Now what?' Now that's a very good question.

CONCLUSION

The Breakdown

"Everyone's a little bit autistic," the tired saying goes. At best, it comes from a misplaced desire to suggest autism is not so much of an outlier or alien concept as they might think it is – to appear empathetic and to strike some common ground. At worst, it's an invalidating ignorance of the lived experience of autistic people and the barriers they can face.

The autism spectrum is best illustrated as a circle comprising several sections (such as eye contact and stimming) on which a person can be anywhere between the outer and inner circumferences, as opposed to a linear diagram which does not account for the full breadth and makeup of the condition.

Of course, non-autistic people may identify with *some* autistic traits, but not to the extent that it causes "significant impairment in social, occupational, or other important areas of current functioning", per the DSM-5. It doesn't negate the fact that autistic people have a different neurology, either.

To use another condition as an example, research has shown that the overwhelming majority of us experience intrusive thoughts from time to time (in their 2014 paper, Radomsky et al. gave the figure at just over 93%), though not everyone will have them to the same distressing and debilitating extent as those with obsessive compulsive disorder (OCD). This is why those who suggest they are a "little bit OCD" over their desire to be clean and organized frustrates OCD sufferers like me, because it's not the same as having constant intrusive thoughts about causing harm to those closest to you if you don't act on a compulsion.

All of the above serves as a disclaimer of sorts for what follows. The principles the industry needs to uphold in order to address the challenges facing autism research (honesty, inclusion, morality, accountability and more, all explored in this chapter) are the same values that could do with being strengthened in society more broadly. They are also key morals for many autistic people, at the foundation of our robust understanding of right and wrong.

This observation does not give credence to the inaccurate claim that we are all "a little bit autistic" simply because we share these common values (this phrase often relies on the incorrect notion that the autism spectrum ranges from allistic to autistic, when in actuality, the spectrum concerns the extent to which different autistic traits manifest in an individual, with a diagnosis given when multiple traits have a significant impact on a person's life). Instead, these innate principles acquire *new* depths of understanding from autistic people as they navigate, examine and deconstruct the social cues they can have difficulty recognizing, and which are so tightly wedded to these standards.

In other words, we can all stand to benefit from the scrutiny of societal constructs from autistic people.

However, one idea not yet explored in depth in this book is our innate and fundamental understanding of right and wrong (even when some studies will suggest we apparently lack this basic understanding of morals and/or empathy). The contributions from multiple autistic advocates within these pages also demonstrate that we know when considerable harm and injustices have been committed against our community, and that some autism researchers are yet to properly recognize and confront this.

Academics are not completely to blame, though. In fact, no one body is responsible for the significant collapse in trust in autism research.

When we talk about trust, we also indulge ourselves in discussions about communication – that has broken down too, and produced a ripple effect of problems across the whole industry. So much of this boils down to either miscommunication, or no communication at all – such as in the form of participation.

If we return to Andrew Wakefield, then we see a disgraced individual who exploited a lack of communication from the medical establishment around outcomes for autistic children post-diagnosis, to intervene and present his own narrative to anxious parents.

Controversial papers, of course, preclude his 1998 study – look no further than the work of Lovaas – but Wakefield emboldened and strengthened the messages around autistic children and interventions, as well as the amount of control the parent lobby has around that narrative. The remnants of Wakefield's work remain, and autism researchers are trying to communicate their own take on what autism is to counteract that. Evidently, that isn't working as well as it could – and should – be, and the autistic community's faith in autism research continues to be tested.

There are too many examples of a widespread communication breakdown, and it's important to underscore how a lack of meaningful consultation can feed into such a crisis.

Looking at grant bodies, Dr Kelsey Martin of the Simons Foundation wasn't the only interviewee to tell me that communication and the vocabulary of institutions was an issue, and that extends to the funding organizations too. Community engagement will enable such organizations to share details of studies they've supported financially using more accessible language.

While questions and scepticism still remain as to why the Spectrum 10K study team's summary of the research differs from the description listed on the grant award shared by the Wellcome Trust, this demonstrates a domino effect where communication can continue to break down. Look no further than the Wellcome Trust only now devising principles on inclusive research, and the National Institutes of Health only concerning themselves with the inclusion of "minorities, women and children" when it is "applicable", rather than with every study. Researchers are far more likely to ignore meaningful engagement in their studies if it is not underscored by bodies with the power to halt or change a study in its very early stages.

Research ethics committees and organizations also possess such an authority, though it's evident they lack a certain amount of bite. The HRA spoke of how frustrated their committees can be with studies lacking meaningful consultation, because they are considered too valuable to reject on the basis of community participation, and how they're seeking to inform researchers of the need to involve the relevant communities as early in the process as possible. There's an acknowledgement that greater diversity is needed in these committees, perhaps bolstered by collaborations with charities, and this would be another way in which autistic people can comment on a study without necessarily participating in it.

Another issue that no doubt sparks exasperation from research ethics bodies is a lack of enforcement around basic academic principles. Patient and public involvement is detailed in the UK's Policy Framework for Health and Social Care research, which draws upon existing legislation, but there is no law in place currently that mandates community engagement, and even then – as the HRA's Barbara Molony-Oates notes – this could only encourage tokenistic inclusion.

Here lies a significant challenge, in that an agreed definition is being pushed by research bodies, but the moment that is enshrined into law or policy documents as something to accomplish, rather than a matter of instinct, then it gives rise to tickbox exercises. What should be an organic process unrestrained by bureaucracy risks becoming formulaic and monolithic, when we just need these conversations to happen.

Meaningful engagement is not about speaking to X number of autistic people or X number of charities, but rather an attitude to what is a fundamental part of research, and an institutional ethos undoubtedly takes a considerable amount of time to change.

The autistic community, however, is clear on what proper participation looks like, and this book has encapsulated a few descriptions. Researchers should take them on board.

Not only that, but research journals have an opportunity to demonstrate in practice what good participatory research looks like, as we heard from *Autism* editor-in-chief Professor Sue Fletcher-Watson. They too can contribute to the communication breakdown we've seen present itself across multiple institutions involved in autism research. In this case, lay abstracts are inaccessible (be it because they use vocabulary that is unfamiliar to most people, or otherwise), the publication processes are not as transparent as they could or should be, and journals could well embrace new technologies through which they can communicate study information – such as through shortform videos. Opening up the freedom of choice around how we receive details about a paper is a key step to ensuring as much of the autistic community can access – and therefore, scrutinize – research as possible.

This is another instance where the autistic community must unpack the politics involved with papers included in research journals. In particular, we must accept a confirmatory statement that reveals the involvement of neurodivergent people in a study, but also masks their identity so as to prevent the "outing" of their diagnosis. It isn't the first instance I've come across where a demand for work to be carried out by members of the community it is about has raised important points about the risk of forcing individuals to reveal personal information about themselves.

There are, of course, protected characteristics, and we can absolutely find a way in which we can ensure community involvement – either in the study team or participants – while respecting privacy. It relates back to what we have explored around not restricting autism research to just autistic researchers, in order to challenge bias and allow for a range of different opinions. To summarize a point made by Professor Fletcher-Watson, sometimes these negative studies produced by allistic researchers can prompt revolutionary papers from autistic academics.

By no means am I arguing that science should be completely devoid of politics. In his 2022 book *Control* Dr Adam Rutherford argues how genetics is political in its very nature, and when we're talking about conducting research on a marginalized community, politics is inevitable. However, autistic people must not be too restrictive so as to constrain allyship or prevent promising developments in the field that are borne from problematic studies. To effectively process the damage done to our community is to realize that we must not completely exclude allistic researchers from autism research.

In fact, interviewees were pretty clear in stating that barring non-autistic researchers would be counter-productive, not least in terms of having an allistic voice to interrogate any bias which may come from autistic researchers studying autistic people. What's important is that allistic academics uplift the autistic community both in the study team and study design. It is far more effective for allies to have a platform and know how to support autistic people in that work, than to advocate for allies – both existing and potential – to be stripped of their positions altogether.

After all, that is what allyship is: to have those outside a marginalized community use their privilege and platforms, which these oppressed individuals do not have, to elevate that community.

Non-autistic researchers must also confront the 'allistic irony' present in their community. Allistic academics have long perpetuated stereotypes and generalizations about autistic people and communication, but are guilty of miscommunication when it comes to sharing information about their papers and studies, with their specific vocabulary being a factor in this confusion. Not only that, but when another characterization of autistic people is that they are reluctant to change, some allistic researchers are unwilling to adopt new ideas or adjust their mindset, often because to do so means to acknowledge a potentially damaging legacy.

How do we address such an attitude? Co-production, naturally, feels like part of the solution – especially if that process allows for the creation of mutually agreed definitions surrounding the work in question. It's hard for miscommunication to occur when both parties are on the same page, as it were.

Equally, such conversations can allow both sides to explain their reasoning and approaches to an issue, hopefully in a civil manner. In the end, they might not agree on the issues at hand, but the researchers may be more receptive to changing their opinion or understanding (or at the very least, start to begin that process) if they speak to autistic people from the very beginning, rather than at any other point – especially at the end, when the community will rightly be frustrated at their inclusion being considered an afterthought.

Ideally, many more studies will be led by autistic researchers alone in time. Until then, a partnership approach is the first step towards centring autistic researchers more often, and giving them greater control of the narrative around autism.

The role of charities can also be caught up in the politics of autism, not least in terms of their leadership and whether the organization is autistic-led. If we can put aside this issue of contention for one moment, then we can turn to the role of charitable organizations as "translators" in the sense of autism research. They are able to go some way in guiding academics on the language they use around autism, as well as help improve the diversity of a study.

When researchers distance themselves from the language of the community – as charity representatives told me they so often do – these organizations are the ones to reframe the findings of a paper in a way that is recognizable to the demographic they represent. Some charities even make it much easier for researchers to get it right, by compiling documents outlining the research priorities emphasized by community members, yet some academics still seem to ignore these publications.

The benefits of researchers and advocates establishing priorities and agreed definitions together are many, but charities can certainly facilitate such conversations, and draw upon a wider community of autistic people and insights. Tim Nicholls of NAS was clear that this doesn't serve a cosmetic or aesthetic purpose, but demonstrates respect – another buzzword that regularly comes up in conversations about establishing trust.

There will no doubt continue to be disagreements and debate over the level of involvement charities should have in contributing to research discussions – especially, as stated above, those led by non-autistic individuals which are not as community-driven as disabled persons organizations (DPOs). However, it is surely in a charity's best interests to seek to make the language and objectives of an autism study accessible to participants at the start of the process, rather than just at the very end when the findings are published. Less "translation" is required by charities if they play a part in the study's communication strategy from the outset.

As this book repeatedly makes clear, such involvement just isn't happening at the level it should be, and the spate of charities having to rush to "translate" study findings at the very end of the process is symptomatic of this disregard towards meaningful involvement from autism researchers.

Equally, as much as the science is political, politicians are dependent on research to inform policy, and it isn't exactly helpful when misunderstandings are an issue here, too.

One of the few politicians who responded to my enquiries – Representative Jessica Benham from Texas – warned of a risk of non-experts misinterpreting research. At other stages, a misunderstanding of a study can fuel friction among autistic advocates, or hinder grant and ethics applications. When politicians help cement the narrative around autism through legislation, the ramifications of such confusion can prove catastrophic for generations, and thus the need for clear vocabulary around a study could not be more important for our policymakers.

We must also hope that while researchers continue to have an issue with considering the simple fact that autism continues into adulthood, politicians are more alert to this reality, and could very well put pressure on academia to generate more papers on this issue.

Yet while research journals, predominantly, amplify papers to fellow academics, it is news outlets that are – in their very nature – focused on disseminating information to the wider public. Frustratingly, it appears the same issues that underpinned the devastating MMR moral panic (to go full circle) continue unchallenged all these years later. The insidious, amorphous autism which was painted as being separate to the individual is still largely framed as a negative and something to be pitied in mainstream coverage.

Similarly, as certain multiply marginalized autistic people are excluded from research by allistic autism researchers, outlets continue to frame autism through one particular demographic, rather than as the diverse dynamic it truly is. Much like researchers are often reluctant to embrace change, especially where it means contradicting previously held beliefs, the news media frequently continues to trade in absolutes whereby change and deviation from this established fact in pursuit of newer ideas is shunned and avoided. It fails to represent the individuality in the commonality, as well as the autistic community's rich diversity across multiple additional identities.

This issue is exacerbated by autism researchers who already use a different vocabulary to autistic people in general, but then have to contend with greater cultural differences and terminology among multiply marginalized autistic people. Academics carrying out their studies aren't considering the language and experiences shared in these groups either.

I can't help but wonder if we are in a position where a catastrophic wrong has been done to the autistic community. Trust has been broken, and we are yet to process the emotions behind it. At the same time, researchers are inducted into an institution and groupthink which comes complete with complex, inaccessible terminology. They are struggling to communicate with a demographic that doesn't always find conversations easy – and where miscommunication occurs, emotions are heightened.

Look no further than the tension surrounding genetics-based autism research and the toxic practice of applied behavioural analysis. In keeping with the conversation around communication, the autism research community must confront the lack of a clear definition of what exactly ABA is. There continues to be talk of "new ABA", "ABA lite", Positive Behaviour Support (PBS, which, as Johnston et al. of Auburn University in Alabama write in 2006, "has been substantially influenced by applied behavior analysis") and more, as practitioners seek to redefine the "treatment" in more positive terms.

This, however, creates ambiguity – the smokescreen which allows for harm to take place – and underscores the underlying problem around differing vocabulary and terminology between researchers and autistic people.

Clarity is urgently needed in the ABA industry in this respect, but whether an agreed definition can ever be reached on such a controversial issue will no doubt continue to be a point of contention going forward. Crucially, though, unless progress is made in this area – and, just as importantly, abusive practices, like those taking place at the JRC in Massachusetts, are shut down – trust will only further falter in autism research.

Though, as some interviewees have explained – and it's worth emphasizing – both genetics and ABA can carry specific, limited benefits when rooted in the community and with as much care and consideration as possible. They still, however, come with a heavy response around them (in some respects, rightly so, when harm has taken place and questionable research objectives are made available).

One solution put forward in this book is having an open dialogue at the start of the research journey for autistic people to air grievances, trauma and experiences with a system that has harmed them. These spaces and environments do not just extend to research either, as Dr Amy Gravino's contributions re-ferred to disputes on social media platforms as well – a complex medium for which compromise without face-to-face interaction is becoming increasingly difficult.

When autistic people give a particularly emotional response to research, then it only serves as a perfect opportunity for allistic researchers to dismiss members of the community as irrational or inauthentic in expressing their opinions, paving the way for them to be dehumanized.

Racialized people can't speak openly, passionately and truthfully about their experiences without the risk of falling into the racist trope of appearing "aggressive"; transgender autistic people shared how they were invalidated in their identity because they confound the rigid and outdated perspectives of gender (especially non-binary people); non-speaking autistic people are assumed to lack agency or autonomy altogether; and autistic women face misogyny around positions of power which the industry think should or shouldn't be afforded to them.

The narrow lens with which some autism researchers view the condition (straight, white, cisgender, male) only makes the problem worse. In talking about meaningful consultation and, thus, effective communication, Connor Ward noted that it's about creating an environment where autistic participants can feel they can engage fully. The definitions and descriptions of "meaningful consultation" by interviewees were fairly synonymous: it must be at the very start of the process and the study's development, rather than some final check once everything has been said and done. It should be a *consultation*, not a *confirmation*.

It's about a confidence in oneself to be their true autistic selves, which brings about the power to express themselves freely and to the greatest possible extent. It becomes increasingly difficult to feel this way and to trust academics to handle their concerns with care – nay, impossible – when researchers are denying your identities.

It's notable that Professor Baron-Cohen chose not to engage in direct communication about his research, and when the ARC was approached for a right of reply, they ultimately decided not to engage with the content of this book.

This connects to a broader point about the power of conversation: the power that comes with whom we choose to have a dialogue, the power certain people and institutions have in leading and shaping the narrative, and the power they can exercise in not talking to an individual or community, with few repercussions.

The solution to restoring trust and confidence in autism research isn't just in facilitating more discussions, but in calling out the absence of those that don't take place when they really should. A failure to do so, and a refusal to learn lessons from issues raised within these pages, would be disastrous. The misplaced fear around autism prevalence, amplified by Wakefield amid revised medical criteria leading to more diagnoses, is not too dissimilar from the moral panic around ADHD diagnoses present at the time of writing this conclusion.

"Could an epidemic of [ADHD] be afflicting Britain's adult population?" asked *Daily Mail* journalist John Naish in the first line of a news article from January 2023 – "epidemic", as a reminder, previously being the word of choice to describe the prevalence of autism by Cure Autism Now co-founder Jon Shestack.

A month later, and Max Stephens wrote in *The Telegraph* of "fears teenagers self-diagnose autism and ADHD using TikTok". The BBC's *Access All* podcast on disability issues was criticized for an episode titled "ADHD and the trend of diagnosis by TikTok".

The most alarming development in recent months, though, came in the form of a BBC *Panorama* episode released in May 2023, which said it had "exposed" private ADHD clinics after reporter Rory Carson went undercover and paid for a private assessment.

The ADHD Foundation responded by saying it was a "poorly researched, sensationalist piece of television journalism" which failed to "capture the historic inequality of access to health services and lack of priority given to patients with ADHD".

Fellow charity ADHD Aware, like the ADHD Foundation, acknowledged that the practices of certain private healthcare providers should be challenged, but also criticized the programme for neglecting to cite reasons for a rise in ADHD diagnoses – such as "a wider improved understanding of how ADHD affects different individuals", and the increasing strain on the NHS causing individuals to pursue private alternatives.

It's all out of the same playbook. Concerns over a nefarious entity (in this case, TikTok) sparking an "epidemic" of diagnoses in young people and adults, amplified by the media, without properly acknowledging advances in the medical field that have likely contributed to that. ADHD in adults wasn't properly recognized by the UK health guidance body NICE until 2008, for example.

When communication breaks down, it becomes a free-for-all for communities and institutions – with the platforms they have available – to establish a prevailing narrative. When trust collapses, it then falls to all parties involved to seek to rebuild that confidence based on equitable criteria. Again, ambiguity can provide the cover for harm and exploitation to be enacted without proper accountability.

So, in this final chapter, let's be clear in consolidating the framework for rebuilding trust in autism research that has been examined across this book, and which is very much implied in its very title.

By working within clearly defined parameters around how trust is established, the ability to measure progress in building community relations, secure parity and reduce abuse becomes much easier – objectives that autism research is still yet to meet, which is only amplifying the distrust felt by autistic people.

There is, therefore, a compelling argument to re-establish the conditions in which trust can be secured, and a potential case – in the "post-truth" world in which we currently find ourselves, where social constructs are breaking down and under continuous scrutiny – to expand these out further.

Drawing upon the learnings in this book, it is clear that trust is reliant on the timely communication of full and accurate information, with a reciprocity that ensures every person is heard (including multiply marginalized individuals), and accepts that some power must be afforded to those without privilege to empower them to discuss ideas openly and make the necessary changes.

It's about understanding that these changes will take place as the working relationship evolves, and embracing them – prioritizing the safety of all parties and acknowledging when harm has been caused in a way that is completely transparent.

Timely information. Reciprocity. Understanding and embracing change. Safety and security. Transparency.

I didn't intend for these principles to be easily abbreviated to TRUST, but it probably helps the book that they can. It's also immensely satisfying to an autistic individual with an affinity for wordplay.

Members of the autistic community have to implement countless coping strategies in order to navigate societal challenges. If the autism research industry wants to overcome its own barriers and win back autistic people's trust – which I certainly believe it can, based on the evidence unearthed here – then it's about time it implemented a strategy of its own.

The blueprint is right here.

References

Introduction

Alldred, M. J., Granholm, A., Hendrix, J., Martini, A. C. and Patterson, D. (2021) Aging with Down syndrome – where are we now and where are we going? *Journal of Clinical Medicine*. Available from: www.ncbi.nlm.nih.gov/pmc/articles/PMC8539670.

Gove, M. (2016, 3 June) EU: In or Out? Sky News [Video file]. Available from: www.youtube.com/live/t8D8AoC-5i8.

National Institute on Aging (2020) Alzheimer's Disease in People with Down Syndrome. Available from: www.nia.nih.gov/health/alzheimers-disease-people-down-syndrome.

Chapter 1: In the Wake of Wakefield

American Psychiatric Association (1980) *Diagnostic and Statistical Manual of Mental Disorders: DSM-III*. Washington, DC: American Psychiatric Association.

American Psychiatric Association (1994) *Diagnostic and Statistical Manual of Mental Disorders: DSM-IV*. Washington, DC: American Psychiatric Association.

American Psychiatric Association (2013) *Diagnostic and Statistical Manual of Mental Disorders: DSM-5*. Washington, DC: American Psychiatric Association.

BBC News (1998, 27 February) Child vaccine linked to autism. Available from: http://news.bbc.co.uk/1/hi/uk/60510.stm.

Czech, H. (2018) Hans Asperger, National Socialism, and "race hygiene" in Nazi-era Vienna. *Molecular Autism*, 9(29). Available from: https://doi.org/10.1186/s13229-018-0208-6.

Deer, B. (2020) *The Doctor Who Fooled the World: Andrew Wakefield's War on Vaccines*. London: Scribe Publications.

Doshi-Velez, F., Avillach, P., Palmer, N., Bousvaros, A. et al. (2015) Prevalence of inflammatory bowel disease among patients with autism spectrum disorders. *Inflammatory Bowel Diseases*, 21(10), 2281–2288. Available from: https://academic.oup.com/ibdjournal/article/21/10/2281/4644914.

Frith, U. (ed.) (1991) *Autism and Asperger Syndrome*. Cambridge: Cambridge University Press.

General Medical Council (2010) *Dr Andrew Jeremy Wakefield: Determination on Serious Professional Misconduct (SPM) and Sanction.* London: General Medical Council. Available from: www.circare.org/autism/Wakefield_SPM_and_SANCTION_32595267.pdf.

Hilton, S., Petticrew, M. and Hunt, K. (2007) Parents' champions vs. vested interests: Who do parents believe about MMR? A qualitative study. *BMC Public Health*, 7(42). Available from: https://bmcpublichealth.biomedcentral.com/articles/10.1186/1471-2458-7-42.

Kanner, L. (1943) Autistic disturbances of affective contact. *Nervous Child*, 2, 217–250.

Laurance, J. (1998, 25 March) Children's vaccine is safe, say experts. *The Independent.* Available from: www.independent.co.uk/news/children-s-vaccine-is-safe-say-experts-1152243.html.

Lee, M., Krishnamurthy, J., Susi, A., Sullivan, C. et al. (2018) Association of autism spectrum disorders and inflammatory bowel disease. *Journal of Autism and Developmental Disorders*, 48, 1523–1529. Available from: https://link.springer.com/article/10.1007/s10803-017-3409-5.

Lombardi, L., Le Clerc, S., Wu, C. L., Bouassida, J. et al. (2023) A human leukocyte antigen imputation study uncovers possible genetic interplay between gut inflammatory processes and autism spectrum disorders. *Translational Psychiatry*, 13, 244.

Manouilenko, I. and Bejerot, S. (2015) Sukhareva – prior to Asperger and Kanner. *Nordic Journal of Psychiatry*, 69(6), 1761–1764.

McElhanon, B. O., McCracken, C., Karpen, S. and Sharp, W. G. (2014) Gastrointestinal symptoms in autism spectrum disorder: A meta-analysis. *Pediatrics*, 133(5), 872–883.

Mirror, The (1998, 12 March) My girl was happy and healthy till she had a routine jab... now she is autistic. p. 39.

NHS Digital (2017) Childhood Vaccination Coverage Statistics – England, 2016–17. Available from: https://digital.nhs.uk/data-and-information/publications/statistical/nhs-immunisation-statistics/childhood-vaccination-coverage-statistics-england-2016-17.

NHS Digital (2022) Childhood Vaccination Coverage Statistics – England, 2021–22. Available from: https://digital.nhs.uk/data-and-information/publications/statistical/nhs-immunisation-statistics/2021-22.

Oxford Reference (2023) Moral panic. Oxford: Oxford University Press. Available from: www.oxfordreference.com/display/10.1093/oi/authority.20110803100208829;jsessionid=A5716C21A6E8989E824D31203D8CF23B.

Roberts, J. (1994, 11 April) Health: Vaccination: do you know the risks? Jan Roberts meets parents who believe immunisation against measles, mumps and rubella injured their children. *The Independent.* Available from: www.independent.co.uk/life-style/health-and-families/health-news/health-vaccination-do-you-know-the-risks-jan-roberts-meets-parents-who-believe-immunisation-against-measles-mumps-and-rubella-injured-their-children-1369519.html.

Russell, G., Stapley, S., Newlove-Delgado, T., Salmon, A. et al. (2021) Time trends in autism diagnosis over 20 years: A UK population-based cohort study. *Journal of Child Psychology and Psychiatry*, 63(6), 674–682. Available from: https://acamh.onlinelibrary.wiley.com/doi/10.1111/jcpp.13505.

Silberman, S. (2015) *Neurotribes: The Legacy of Autism and How to Think Smarter about People Who Think Differently*. London: Allen & Unwin.

TIME (1948, 26 April) Medicine: Frosted children. New York: *TIME*. Available from: https://content.time.com/time/subscriber/article/0,33009,798484,00.html.

UK Health Security Agency (2022) *Around 1 in 10 Children Starting School at Risk of Measles* [Press release]. London: GOV.UK. Available from: www.gov.uk/government/news/around-1-in-10-children-starting-school-at-risk-of-measles.

Wakefield, A., Murch, S. H., Anthony, A., Linnell, J. et al. (1998) RETRACTED: Ileal-lymphoid-nodular hyperplasia, non-specific colitis, and pervasive developmental disorder in children. *The Lancet*, 351(9103), 637–641. Available from: www.thelancet.com/journals/lancet/article/PIIS0140673697110960.

Wing, L. (1981) Asperger's syndrome: A clinical account. *Psychological Medicine*, 11(1), 115–129.

Wing, L. and Gould, J. (1979) Severe impairments of social interaction and associated abnormalities in children: Epidemiology and classification. *Journal of Autism and Developmental Disorders*, 9, 11–29.

World Health Organization (2019) *ICD-11 for Mortality and Morbidity Statistics*. Geneva: World Health Organization. Available from: https://icd.who.int/browse11/l-m/en#/http://id.who.int/icd/entity/437815624.

Chapter 2: The Right to Know

KleefstraSyndrome.org (2017) What Is Kleefstra Syndrome? Available from: www.kleefstrasyndrome.org/what-is-kleefstra-syndrome.

Natri, H. (n.d.) Commentary: Developing a framework for ethical genetic autism research [Pre-print]. Supplied.

Chapter 3: The Allistic Irony

Botha, M. (2021) Academic, activist, or advocate? Angry, entangled, and emerging: A critical reflection on autism knowledge production. *Frontiers in Psychology*, 12. Available from: https://doi.org/10.3389/fpsyg.2021.727542.

Botha, M. and Cage, E. (2022) "Autism research is in crisis": A mixed method study of researcher's constructions of autistic people and autism research. *Frontiers in Psychology*, 13, 1050897. Available from: https://doi.org/10.3389/fpsyg.2022.1050897.

Milton, D. (2018, 2 March) The double empathy problem. National Autistic Society. Available from: www.autism.org.uk/advice-and-guidance/professional-practice/double-empathy.

Singer, A., Lutz, A., Escher, J. and Halladay, A. (2023) A full semantic toolbox is essential for autism research and practice to thrive. *Autism Research*, 16(3), 497–501. Available from: https://onlinelibrary.wiley.com/doi/full/10.1002/aur.2876.

Zamzow, R. (2022, 14 April) Why autism therapies have an evidence problem. *Spectrum*. Available from: www.spectrumnews.org/news/why-autism-therapies-have-an-evidence-problem.

Chapter 4: The Baron-Cohen Legacy

Agelink van Rentergem, J. A., Lever, A. G. and Geurts, H. M. (2019) Negatively phrased items of the Autism Spectrum Quotient function differently for groups with and without autism. *Autism*, 23(7), 1752–1764. Available from: https://journals.sagepub.com/doi/10.1177/1362361319828361.

Anthes, E. (2020, 2 April) Popular autism screening tool is unreliable, study suggests. *Spectrum*. Available from: www.spectrumnews.org/news/popular-autism-screening-tool-is-unreliable-study-suggests.

Baron-Cohen, S. (1990) Autism: A specific cognitive disorder of "mind-blindness". *International Review of Psychiatry*, 2, 81–90.

Baron-Cohen, S. (2002) The extreme male brain theory of autism. *Trends in Cognitive Science*, 6(6), 248–254.

Baron-Cohen, S., Bowen, D. C., Holt, R. J., Allison, C. et al. (2015) The "Reading the Mind in the Eyes" test: Complete absence of typical sex difference in ~400 men and women with autism. *PLOS ONE*, 10(8), e0136521. Available from: https://doi.org/10.1371/journal.pone.0136521.

Baron-Cohen, S., Wheelwright, S., Skinner, R., Martin, J. and Clubby, E. (2001) The Autism Spectrum Quotient (AQ): Evidence from Asperger syndrome/high-functioning autism, males and females, scientists and mathematicians. *Journal of Autism and Developmental Disorders*, 31, 5–17.

Dinishak, J. and Akhtar, N. (2013) A critical examination of mindblindness as a metaphor for autism. *Child Development Perspectives*, 7(2), 110–114.

Duffy, J. and Dorner, R. (2011) The pathos of "mindblindness": Autism, science, and sadness in "theory of mind" narratives. *Journal of Literary and Cultural Disability Studies*, 5, 201–215.

Gernsbacher, M. A. and Yergeau, M. (2019) Empirical failures of the claim that autistic people lack a theory of mind. *Archives of Scientific Psychology*, 7(1), 102–118. Available from: https://doi.org/10.1037/arc0000067.

Greenberg, D. M., Warrier, V., Alison, C. and Baron-Cohen, S. (2018a, 12 November) Extreme male brain theory of autism confirmed in large new study – and no, it doesn't mean autistic people lack empathy or are more "male". *The Conversation*. Available from: https://theconversation.com/extreme-male-brain-theory-of-autism-confirmed-in-large-new-study-and-no-it-doesnt-mean-autistic-people-lack-empathy-or-are-more-male-106800.

Greenberg, D. M., Warrier, V., Allison, C. and Baron-Cohen, S. (2018b) Testing the empathizing-systemizing theory of sex differences and the extreme male brain theory of autism in half a million people. *Proceedings of the National Academy of Sciences of the United States of America*, 115(48), 12152–12157. Available from: https://doi.org/10.1073/pnas.1811032115.

Krahn, T. M. and Fenton, A. (2012) The extreme male brain theory of autism and the potential adverse effects for boys and girls with autism. *Journal of Bioethical Inquiry*, 9, 93–103.

Loomes, R., Hull, L. and Mandy, W. P. L. (2017) What is the male-to-female ratio in autism spectrum disorder? A systematic review and meta-analysis. *Journal of the American Academy of Child and Adolescent Psychiatry*, 56(6), 466–474.

McCarthy, J. (2018, 13 December) Rain Man at 30: Damaging stereotype or "the best thing that happened to autism"? *The Guardian*. Available from: www.theguardian.com/film/2018/dec/13/rain-man-at-30-autism-hoffman-cruise-levinson.

National Autistic Society (2012) *The Way We Are: Autism in 2012*. London: The National Autistic Society. Available from: https://web.archive.org/web/20130208062607/https:/www.autism.org.uk/~/media/20F5BD5ADBDE42479F126C3E550CE5B0.ashx.

Ridley, R. (2019) Some difficulties behind the concept of the "extreme male brain" in autism research. A theoretical review. *Research in Autism Spectrum Disorders*, 57, 19–27.

Taylor, E., Livingston, L., Clutterbuck, R. and Shah, P. (2020) Psychometric concerns with the 10-item Autism Spectrum Quotient (AQ10) as a measure of trait autism in the general population. *Experimental Results*, 1, E3. Available from: https://doi.org/10.1017/exp.2019.3.

Chapter 5: The Art of Consultation

Academic Autism Spectrum Partnership in Research and Education (2020) About. Available from: https://aaspire.org/about.

Autism Independent UK (2021) Sexuality and Autism © TEACCH Report. Available from: https://autismuk.com/autism/sexuality-and-autism/teacch-report.

Baron-Cohen, S. (2021) Study: Spectrum 10K – Common Variant Genetics of Autism and Autistic Traits (GWAS) Consortium [letter from Simon Baron-Cohen to Health Research Authority]. Available from: https://thelifeofathinker.files.wordpress.com/2022/06/spectrum-10k-hra-response.pdf.

BBC Breakfast (2021, 24 August) Professor Simon Baron-Cohen's interview with BBC Breakfast [Twitter]. Available from: https://twitter.com/BBCBreakfast/status/1430076275020943375.

Boycott Spectrum 10K (2021) Plain text of the full Boycott Spectrum 10K statement. Aucademy. Available from: https://aucademy.co.uk/2021/09/04/plain-text-of-the-full-boycott-s10k-statement.

British Neuroscience Association (2019) Research Assistant Autism – University of Cambridge. Available from: www.bna.org.uk/jobs/job/research-assistant-autism-university-of-cambridge.

Buckle, L. (2022) Spectrum 10K Consultation: Introducing Leneh Buckle, Co-Lead, HVM. Hopkins Van Mil. Available from: www.hopkinsvanmil.co.uk/news/2022/8/7/spectrum-10k-consultation-introducing-leneh-buckle-co-lead-hvm.

Health Research Authority (2021, 2022) Spectrum 10K, How the HRA Manages Your Feedback. London: Health Research Authority. Available from: www.hra.nhs.uk/about-us/news-updates/spectrum-10k-how-hra-manages-your-feedback.

Health Research Authority (2022) Spectrum 10K Update – 20 May 2022. Available from: www.hra.nhs.uk/about-us/governance/feedback-raising-concerns/spectrum-10k-update-19-may-2022.

Hopkins Van Mil (2022a) *Spectrum 10K Phase 1: Planning Phase 2 – The Consultation Co-design*. Available from: www.hopkinsvanmil.co.uk/spectrum-10k-consultation.

Hopkins Van Mil (2022b) *Spectrum 10K Consultation – Phase 2: The Co-design*. Available from: www.hopkinsvanmil.co.uk/spectrum-10k-consultation.

Hopkins Van Mil (2023a) *Transcript of the Webinar 1 Questions and Answers. Topic: Aims of the Study*. Available from: www.hopkinsvanmil.co.uk/spectrum-10k-the-consultation.

Hopkins Van Mil (2023b) *Transcript of the Webinar 2 Questions and Answers. Topic: Ethics and Values.* Available from: www.hopkinsvanmil.co.uk/spectrum-10k-the-consultation.

Hopkins Van Mil (2023c) *Transcript of the Webinar 4 Questions and Answers. Topic: Data Collection and Management.* Available from: www.hopkinsvanmil.co.uk/spectrum-10k-the-consultation.

Hopkins van Mil (2023d) *Transcript of the Webinar 5 Questions and Answers. Topic: Any Other Topics about Improving or Changing the Spectrum 10K Study.* Available from: www.hopkinsvanmil.co.uk/spectrum-10k-the-consultation.

Legislation.gov.uk (2016) *Regulation (EU) 2016/679 of the European Parliament and of the Council.* Available from: www.legislation.gov.uk/eur/2016/679/article/24.

Nicolaidis, C., Raymaker, D., Kapp, S. K., Baggs, A. et al. (2019) The AASPIRE practice-based guidelines for the inclusion of autistic adults in research as co-researchers and study participants. *Autism*, 23(8), 2007–2019. Available from: www.ncbi.nlm.nih.gov/pmc/articles/PMC6776684.

O'Dell, L. (2021a, 29 August) What is the Spectrum 10K DNA study into autism – and why are autistic people concerned? *indy100*. Available from: www.indy100.com/news/spectrum-10k-study-autism-dna-b1910619.

O'Dell, L. (2021b, 30 November) Spectrum 10K: Health Research Authority's request for further information about autism study revealed. Available from: https://liamodell.com/2021/11/30/spectrum-10k-study-autism-genetics-dna-simon-baron-cohen-university-of-cambridge-health-research-authority.

O'Dell, L. (2021c, 15 December) Spectrum 10K: Controversial autism study considered £10,000 "prize draw" to encourage participants. Available from: https://liamodell.com/2021/12/15/spectrum-10k-autism-dna-genetics-research-simon-baron-cohen-wellcome-trust-cambridge-autism-research-centre-eugenics.

O'Dell, L. (2022a, 10 March) Spectrum 10K: Website for controversial study mentions ABA and "autistically handicapped" charities. Available from: https://liamodell.com/2022/03/10/spectrum-10k-autism-dna-simon-baron-cohen-cambridge-university-research-genetics-charities-health-research-authority.

O'Dell, L. (2022b, 16 November) Spectrum 10K: Researchers warn NHS Trust not to respond to Twitter "trolls" criticising autism DNA study. Available from: https://liamodell.com/2021/11/16/spectrum-10k-autism-dna-research-study-university-of-cambridge-genetics-nhs.

O'Dell, L. (2022c, 18 November) Spectrum 10K: NHS Trust paused involvement in autism study following staff "anxieties", email reveals. Available from: https://liamodell.com/2022/11/18/leicester-partnership-nhs-trust-spectrum-10k-autism-dna-study-cambridge-simon-baron-cohen.

O'Dell, L. (2022d, 12 April) Spectrum 10K: Another email sees autism researchers criticise "trolls" targeting controversial DNA study. Available from: https://liamodell.com/2022/04/12/spectrum-10k-trolls-cambridge-health-research-authority-autism-consultation-genetics-dna-study.

O'Dell, L. (2022e, 31 March) Spectrum 10K: Autism study team "cannot continue to respond" to journalist's requests. Available from: https://liamodell.com/2022/03/31/spectrum-10k-study-dna-autism-genetics-cambridge-research-simon-baron-cohen-health-research-authority.

O'Dell, L. (2022f, 28 April) Spectrum 10K "expected to re-launch in May", meeting minutes suggest. Available from: https://liamodell.com/2022/04/28/

spectrum-10k-autism-research-centre-university-of-cambridge-dna-simon-baron-cohen-genetics.

O'Dell, L. (2022g, 2 June) Spectrum 10K: Study team's response to Health Research Authority's enquiries revealed. Available from: https://liamodell.com/2022/06/02/spectrum-10k-study-autism-dna-genetics-health-research-authority-investigation-consultation-autism-research-centre-cambridge-cure-autism-now-autism-speaks.

O'Dell, L. (2023, 23 May) Spectrum 10K: Consultation co-designers should agree to "improve the study, not stop it". Available from: https://liamodell.com/2022/05/23/spectrum-10k-consultation-hopkins-van-mil-health-research-authority-ambassadors.

Special Olympics (2023) Why the R-Word is the R-Slur. Available from: www.specialolympics.org/stories/impact/why-the-r-word-is-the-r-slur.

Spectrum 10K (2021) Statement – 10th September. https://web.archive.org/web/20220924194605/https://spectrum10k.org/statement-10th-september.

Spectrum 10K (2022) Consultation Update. https://web.archive.org/web/20221006061400/https://spectrum10k.org/consultation-update.

Spectrum 10K (2023a) Summary of the Spectrum 10K Consultation (2021–2023). Available from: https://web.archive.org/web/20230929142127/https://spectrum10k.org/summary-of-the-spectrum-10k-consultation.

Spectrum 10K (2023b) Phase 3 Consultation Update – 2nd June 2023. Available from: https://web.archive.org/web/20230929134025/https://spectrum10k.org/phase-3-consultation-update.

Spectrum 10K (n.d.) Frequently Asked Questions. Available from: https://web.archive.org/web/20230929135619/https://spectrum10k.org/faqs/genetic-data.

University of Cambridge (2020) IRAS Form. Available from: https://thelifeofathinker.files.wordpress.com/2021/10/1c.-iras_form_03062020_redacted.pdf.

University of Cambridge (n.d.) Collaborative Award in Science – preliminary application. Available from: https://gizmonaut.net/autism-documents/Spectrum10K-research-application-pre-submission.pdf.

Ward, C. (2021, 24 August) Connor Ward's conversation with Spectrum 10K [Twitter]. Available from: https://x.com/ConnorWardUK/status/1430125833184743424?s=20.

Wellcome Sanger Institute (2019, 15 October) Sanger Institute refutes allegations of misuse of African DNA data from partner institutions. Available from: www.sanger.ac.uk/news_item/sanger-institute-refutes-allegations-misuse-african-dna-data-partner-institutions.

Wellcome Sanger Institute (n.d.) Professor Matthew Hurles, FMedSci, FRS. Available from: www.sanger.ac.uk/person/hurles-matthew.

Chapter 6: The Invisible

Baron-Cohen, S. (2002) The extreme male brain theory of autism. *Trends in Cognitive Science*, 6(6), 248–254.

Botha, M. and Gillespie-Lynch, K. (2022) Come as you are: Examining autistic identity development and the neurodiversity movement through an intersectional lens. *Human Development*, 66(2), 93–112. Available from: https://doi.org/10.1159/000524123.

Boyd, B. A., Hume, K. A., Jaramillo, M. E., Luelmo, P. et al. (2022) Patterns in reporting and participant inclusion related to race and ethnicity in autism intervention literature: Data from a large-scale systematic review of evidence-based practices. *Autism*, 26(8), 2026–2040. Available from: https://journals.sagepub.com/doi/10.1177/13623613211072593.

Coombs, C. B. (2020, 22 October) What it's like to be a Black autism researcher [Podcast]. *Spectrum*. Available from: www.spectrumnews.org/features/multimedia/podcasts/spectrum-stories/what-its-like-to-be-a-black-autism-researcher.

Chapter 7: The Translators

Autism Speaks (2016) I Am Autism commercial by Autism Speaks [Video file]. Available from: https://youtu.be/9UgLnWJFGHQ.

Autism Speaks (2018) *Annual Report 2018*. Princeton, NJ: Autism Speaks. Available from: www.autismspeaks.org/sites/default/files/2018_annual_report.pdf.

Autism Speaks (2021) *April 2020–March 2021: Annual Report*. Princeton, NJ: Autism Speaks. Available from: www.autismspeaks.org/sites/default/files/2021_annual_report.pdf.

Autism Speaks (n.d.) About Autism Speaks. Available from: www.autismspeaks.org/about-autism-speaks.

Autism Speaks (n.d.) Questions and Answers. Available from: www.autismspeaks.org/autism-speaks-questions-answers-facts.

Autistic Self Advocacy Network (n.d.) *ASAN Statement on Genetic Research and Autism*. Washington, DC: Autistic Self Advocacy Network. Available from: https://autisticadvocacy.org/wp-content/uploads/2022/03/genetic-statement.pdf.

Autistica (2016) *Your Questions: Shaping Future Autism Research*. London: Autistica. Available from: www.autistica.org.uk/downloads/files/Autism-Top-10-Your-Priorities-for-Autism-Research.pdf.

Fox, A. (2016, 18 October) Why Autism Speaks dropped the word "cure" from its mission statement. *Huffington Post*. Available from: www.huffingtonpost.co.uk/entry/cure-for-autism_n_58062f2be4b0dd54ce3522b1.

Chapter 8: 'Fixed'

Association for Behavior Analysis International (2022) Position Statement on the Use of CESS. Available from: www.abainternational.org/about-us/policies-and-positions/position-statement-on-the-use-of-cess-2022.aspx.

Autistic Self Advocacy Network (2023) #StopTheShock: The Judge Rotenberg Center, Torture, and How We Can Stop It. Available from: https://autisticadvocacy.org/actioncenter/issues/school/climate/jrc.

Behavior Analyst Certification Board (2020) *Ethics Code for Behavior Analysts*. Available from: www.bacb.com/wp-content/uploads/2022/01/Ethics-Code-for-Behavior-Analysts-230119-a.pdf.

Bonello, C. (2018, 1 October) 11,521 people answered this autism survey. Warning: the results may challenge you. Autistic Not Weird. Available from: https://autisticnotweird.com/2018survey.

Bonello, C. (2022, 23 March) Results and analysis of the Autistic Not Weird 2022 autism survey: The cure question. Autistic Not Weird. Available from: https://autisticnotweird.com/autismsurvey/#cures.

Borenstein, I. (2013) *Report by Monitor Judge Isaac Borenstein (Ret.) for the Judge Rotenberg Educational Center (JRC)*. Massachusetts Attorney General's Office. Available from: www.scribd.com/doc/139810750/Judge-Rotenberg-Center-AG-Report.

Boston25News (2012, 17 May) Graphic video of teen being restrained, shocked played in court. Available from: www.boston25news.com/news/graphic-video-of-teen-being-restrained-shocked-played-in-court/138330674.

Botha, M., Chapman, R., Giwa Onaiwu, M., Kapp, S. K., Stannard Ashley, A. and Walker, N. (2024) The neurodiversity concept was developed collectively: An overdue correction on the origins of neurodiversity theory. *Autism*. Available from: https://doi.org/10.1177/13623613241237871.

Bottema-Beutel, K. and Crowley, S. (2021) Pervasive undisclosed conflicts of interest in applied behavior analysis autism literature. *Frontiers in Psychology*, 12, 676303. Available from: https://doi.org/10.3389/fpsyg.2021.676303.

Broderick, A. (2022) *The Autism Industrial Complex: How Branding, Marketing, and Capital Investment Turned Autism into Big Business*. Gorham, ME: Myers Education Press.

Broderick, A. and Roscigno, R. (2021) Autism, Inc.: The Autism Industrial Complex. *Journal of Disability Studies in Education*, 2(1), 77–101. Available from: https://doi.org/10.1163/25888803-bja10008.

Buescher, A. V., Cidav, Z., Knapp, M. and Mandell, D. S. (2014) Costs of autism spectrum disorders in the United Kingdom and the United States. *JAMA Pediatrics*, 168(8), 721–728. Available from: https://doi.org/10.1001/jamapediatrics.2014.210.

Chance, P. (1974) "After you hit a child, you can't just get up and leave him; you are hooked to that kid": A conversation with Ivar Lovaas about self-mutilating children and how their parents make it worse. *Psychology Today*, 7(8), 76–80, 82–84.

Committee on Energy and Commerce (2022) *Report of the Committee on Energy and Commerce to Accompany H.R. 7667*. Washington, DC: US Government Publishing Office. Available from: www.govinfo.gov/content/pkg/CRPT-117hrpt348/html/CRPT-117hrpt348.htm.

Community Research and Development Information Service (2023) Genome, Environment, Microbiome & Metabolome in Autism: An Integrated Multi-omic Systems Biology Approach to Identify Biomarkers for Personalized Treatment and Primary Prevention of Autism Spectr. Brussels: European Commission. Available from: https://cordis.europa.eu/project/id/825033.

Diament, M. (2023, 5 January) Congress approves boost to special ed, disability programs. Disability Scoop. Available from: www.disabilityscoop.com/2023/01/05/congress-approves-boost-to-special-ed-disability-programs/30186.

European Union (2000) EU Charter – Charter of Fundamental Rights of the European Union. *Official Journal of the European Communities*, 43, C 364/9. Available from: www.europarl.europa.eu/charter/pdf/text_en.pdf.

Food and Drug Administration (2020) Banned devices: Electrical stimulation devices for self-injurious or aggressive behavior. *Federal Register*, 85(45), 13312–13354. Available from: www.federalregister.gov/documents/2020/03/06/2020-04328/banned-devices-electrical-stimulation-devices-for-self-injurious-or-aggressive-behavior.

Gentes-Hunt, L. (2011, 26 May) Judge Rotenberg Center's founder responds to in-dictment, allegations. Patch. Available from: https://patch.com/massachusetts/canton/judge-rotenberg-centers-founder-responds-to-indicment4fce86c98d.

Gonnerman, J. (2012, 31 August) 31 shocks later. *New York Magazine*. Available from: https://nymag.com/news/features/andre-mccollins-rotenberg-center-2012-9.

Gorycki, K. A., Ruppel, P. R. and Zane, T. (2020) Is long-term ABA therapy abusive? A response to Sandoval-Norton and Shkedy. *Cogent Psychology*, 7, 1. Available from: https://doi.org/10.1080/23311908.2020.1823615.

Judge Rotenberg Center (2018) *Safeguards for the Use of Aversives with Students at JRC*. Canton, MA: Judge Rotenberg Center. Available from: https://web.archive.org/web/20230111021449/https://www.judgerc.org/assets/jrc_policy_safeguards_for_the_use_of_aversives.pdf.

Judge Rotenberg Center (n.d.) *Misperceptions vs. Realities of the Use of Contingent Skin Shock (CSS) at the Judge Rotenberg Center*. Canton, MA: Judge Rotenberg Center. Available from: https://web.archive.org/web/20221007081940/www.judgerc.org/assets/misperceptions_vs_realities_of_css_at_jrc_2022.pdf.

Kupferstein, H. (2018) Evidence of increased PTSD symptoms in autistics ex-posed to applied behavior analysis. *Advances in Autism*, 4(3). Available from: www.researchgate.net/publication/322239353_Evidence_of_increased_PTSD_symptoms_in_autistics_exposed_to_applied_behavior_analysis.

Leaf, J. B., Ross, R. K., Cihon, J. H. and Weiss, M. J. (2018) Evaluating Kupferstein's claims of the relationship of behavioral intervention to PTSS for individuals with autism. *Advances in Autism*, 4(3), 122–129. Available from: https://doi.org/10.1108/AIA-02-2018-0007.

McFadden, C., Monahan, K. and Kaplan, A. (2021, 28 April) A decades-long fight over an electric shock treatment led to an FDA ban. But the fight is far from over. *NBC News*. Available from: www.nbcnews.com/health/health-care/decades-long-fight-over-electric-shock-treatment-led-fda-ban-n1265546.

Méndez, J. (2013) *Report of the Special Rapporteur on Torture and Other Cruel, Inhu-man or Degrading Treatment or Punishment*. New York: United Nations Gen-eral Assembly. Available from: www.ohchr.org/sites/default/files/Documents/HRBodies/HRCouncil/RegularSession/Session22/A-HRC-22-53-Add4_EFS.pdf.

National Institute for Health and Care Excellence (2020) NICE draft guidance addresses the continuing debate about the best approach to the diagnosis and management of ME/CFS. London: National Institute for Health and Care Excellence. Available from: www.nice.org.uk/news/article/nice-draft-guidance-addresses-the-continuing-debate-about-the-best-approach-to-the-diagnosis-and-management-of-me-cfs.

Office for National Statistics (2021) Updated Estimates of Coronavirus (COV-ID-19) Related Deaths by Disability Status, England: 24 January to 20 Novem-ber 2020. Available from: www.ons.gov.uk/peoplepopulationandcommunity/birthsdeathsandmarriages/deaths/articles/coronaviruscovid19relateddeathsbydisabilitystatusenglandandwales/24januaryto20november2020.

Pilkington, E. (2011, 25 May) Founder of electric shock autism treatment school forced to quit. *The Guardian*. Available from: www.theguardian.com/world/2011/may/25/electric-shock-autism-treatment-school.

Roscigno, R. (2021, 7 July) Your autistic child can have a great life. Here's how. TEDxMileHigh [Video file]. Available from: www.youtube.com/watch?v=5ioacoVxb3w.

Rutherford, A. (2022) *Control: The Dark History and Troubling Present of Eugenics.* London: W&N.

Sandoval-Norton, A. H., Shkedy, G. and Shkedy, D. (2019) How much compliance is too much compliance: Is long-term ABA therapy abuse? *Cogent Psychology*, 6, 1. Available from: https://doi.org/10.1080/23311908.2019.1641258.

Shkedy, G., Shkedy, D. and Sandoval-Norton, A. H. (2021) Long-term ABA therapy is abusive: A response to Gorycki, Ruppel, and Zane. *Advances in Neurodevelopmental Disorders*, 5, 126–134. Available from: https://doi.org/10.1007/s41252-021-00201-1.

Silberman, S. (2015) *Neurotribes: The Legacy of Autism and How to Think Smarter about People Who Think Differently.* London: Allen & Unwin.

Singer, J. (2023) [Blog post]. Available from: https://neurodiversity2.blogspot.com/2023/10/a-factual-response-to-martijn-dekkers.html.

Singer, J. (n.d.) Quotations from my work [Blog post]. Available from: https://neurodiversity2.blogspot.com/p/selected-quotations.html.

SpookyLuka (2023, 20 June) Screenshot of Judy Singer's LinkedIn post [Twitter]. Available from: https://twitter.com/SpookyLuka/status/167099207900530278 7?s=20.

Supreme Judicial Court of Massachusetts (2023) *Judge Rotenberg Educational Center Inc v Commissioner of Department of Developmental Services* (2023). Available from: https://caselaw.findlaw.com/court/ma-supreme-judicial-court/115033716. html.

Troisi, J., Autio, R., Beopoulos, T., Bravaccio, C. et al. (2020) Genome, Environment, Microbiome and Metabolome in Autism (GEMMA) study design: Biomarkers identification for precision treatment and primary prevention of autism spectrum disorders by an integrated multi-omics systems biology approach. *Brain Sciences*, 10(10), 743. Available from: https://doi.org/10.3390/brainsci10100743.

Tung, L. (2022) How a therapy once seen as a victory for autistic kids has come under fire as abuse. WHYY. Available from: https://whyy.org/segments/how-a-therapy-once-seen-as-a-victory-for-autistic-kids-has-come-under-fire-as-abuse.

Undue Effluence (2023, 18 June) Screenshot of Judy Singer's Twitter posts [Twitter]. Available from: https://twitter.com/UndueEffluence/status/16702355017 71763712?s=20.

United States Court of Appeals for the District of Columbia Circuit (2021) *The Judge Rotenberg Educational Center, Inc. v United States Food and Drug Administration et al.* Available from: www.cadc.uscourts.gov/internet/opinions.nsf/C32A7577ED02127D8525870A00555511/$file/20-1087-1905079.pdf.

Vinet, É., Pineau, C. A., Clarke, A. E., Scott, S. et al. (2015) Increased risk of autism spectrum disorders in children born to women with systemic lupus erythematosus: Results from a large population-based cohort. *Arthritis and Rheumatology*, 67(12), 3201–3208. Available from: https://doi.org/10.1002/art.39320.

Williams, R. (2018) Autonomously autistic: Exposing the locus of autistic pathology. *Canadian Journal of Disability Studies*, 7(2), 60–82. Available from: https://doi.org/10.15353/cjds.v7i2.423.

Zarembo, A. (2012, 6 August) Ole Ivar Lovaas dies at 83; UCLA psychology professor pioneered autism treatment. *Los Angeles Times*. Available from: www.

latimes.com/archives/la-xpm-2010-aug-06-la-me-ivar-lovaas-20100806-story.html.

Zerbo, O., Qian, Y., Yoshida, C., Grether, J. K., Van de Water, J. and Croen, L. A. (2015) Maternal infection during pregnancy and autism spectrum disorders. *Journal of Autism and Developmental Disorders*, 45, 4015–4025.

Chapter 9: Cheques and Balances

Autistic Self Advocacy Network (2022, 14 February) Open letter to the Lancet Commission on the future of care and clinical research in autism. Available from: https://autisticadvocacy.org/2022/02/open-letter-to-the-lancet-commission-on-the-future-of-care-and-clinical-research-in-autism.

Dattaro, L. (2023, 18 July) "A catalyst for change": NIH makes first call for research supporting minimally verbal autistic people. *Spectrum*. Available from: www.spectrumnews.org/news/a-catalyst-for-change-nih-makes-first-call-for-research-supporting-minimally-verbal-autistic-people.

Health Research Authority (2023a) UK Policy Framework for Health and Social Care Research. Available from: www.hra.nhs.uk/planning-and-improving-research/policies-standards-legislation/uk-policy-framework-health-social-care-research/uk-policy-framework-health-and-social-care-research.

Health Research Authority (2023b) Putting People First – Embedding Public Involvement in Health and Social Care Research. Available from: www.hra.nhs.uk/planning-and-improving-research/best-practice/public-involvement/putting-people-first-embedding-public-involvement-health-and-social-care-research.

Interagency Autism Coordinating Committee (n.d.) Overview. US Department of Health and Human Services. Available from: https://iacc.hhs.gov/about-iacc.

Kern Koegel, L. (2023) Editorial – February 2022. *Journal of Autism and Developmental Disorders*, 53, 515. Available from: https://link.springer.com/article/10.1007/s10803-023-05899-7.

Lancet, The (2023) Publishing Excellence. Available from: www.thelancet.com/publishing-excellence.

Lord, C., Havdahl, A., Carbone, P., Anagnostou, E. et al. (2022) The Lancet Commission on the future of care and clinical research in autism. *The Lancet Commissions*, 399(10321), 271–334.

National Institute on Deafness and Other Communication Disorders (2023a, April) Notice of Special Interest (NOSI): Promoting Language and Communication in Minimally Verbal/Non-Speaking Individuals with Autism. National Institutes of Health. Available from: https://grants.nih.gov/grants/guide/notice-files/NOT-DC-23-009.html.

National Institute on Deafness and Other Communication Disorders (2023b, July) Request for Information (RFI): Inviting Input Regarding NIDCD's Research Directions to Support Communication in Minimally Verbal/Non-Speaking People. National Institutes of Health. Available from: https://grants.nih.gov/grants/guide/notice-files/NOT-DC-23-013.html.

National Institutes of Health (2021) Peer Review. Bethesda, MA: National Institutes of Health. Available from: https://grants.nih.gov/grants/peer-review.htm.

Spectrum (2022) Your questions about the *Lancet* Commission and "profound autism," answered. Available from: www.spectrumnews.org/opinion/q-and-a/your-questions-about-the-lancet-commission-and-profound-autism-answered.

UK Standards for Public Involvement (2019) UK Standards for Public Involvement. National Institute for Health and Care Research. Available from: https://sites.google.com/nihr.ac.uk/pi-standards/standards.

Chapter 10: Political Persuasion

Autism Speaks (2022a) *Impacting Lives: Annual Report: April 2021–March 2022.* Princeton, NJ: Autism Speaks. Available from: www.autismspeaks.org/sites/default/files/2022_annual_report.pdf.

Autism Speaks (2022b, 1 February) ABA is now covered by Texas Medicaid [Twitter]. Available from: https://twitter.com/autismvotes/status/1488618157908627456?s=20.

Autistic Self Advocacy Network (2007, 8 December) Comments at November 30, 2007 IACC Meeting. Available from: https://autisticadvocacy.org/2007/12/comments-at-november-30-2007-iacc-meeting.

Bush, G. W. (2006) President's Statement on Combating Autism Act of 2006. Washington: Office of the Press Secretary, The White House. Available from: https://georgewbush-whitehouse.archives.gov/news/releases/2006/12/20061219-1.html.

Department of Health (2010) *"Fulfilling and Rewarding Lives": The Strategy for Adults with Autism in England.* London: Department of Health. Available from: https://webarchive.nationalarchives.gov.uk/ukgwa/20130104203954/http://www.dh.gov.uk/en/Publicationsandstatistics/Publications/PublicationsPolicyAndGuidance/DH_113369.

Department of Health and Social Care (2021) *The National Strategy for Autistic Children, Young People and Adults: 2021 to 2026.* London: GOV.UK. Available from: https://assets.publishing.service.gov.uk/government/uploads/system/uploads/attachment_data/file/1004528/the-national-strategy-for-autistic-children-young-people-and-adults-2021-to-2026.pdf.

House of Commons Committee on Standards (2022) *All-Party Parliamentary Groups: Improving Governance and Regulation.* London: UK Parliament. Available from: https://committees.parliament.uk/publications/22081/documents/163809/default.

O'Keefe, E. (2006, 7 December) Congress declares war on autism. *ABC News.* Available from: https://abcnews.go.com/Health/story?id=2708925.

Piney Jr, J. J. (2015) *The Politics of Autism: Navigating the Contested Spectrum.* London: Rowman & Littlefield.

Pitney, J. (2016, 11 March) John Pitney: The politics of autism [Video file]. Richard Nixon Foundation. Available from: https://youtu.be/0KakbQmTHf0.

Chapter 11: Pressing Matters

Department for Work and Pensions (2024) Family Resources Survey: Financial year 2022 to 2023. Available from: www.gov.uk/government/

statistics/family-resources-survey-financial-year-2022-to-2023/family-resources-survey-financial-year-2022-to-2023#self-employment-1.

Karaminis, T., Gabrielatos, C., Maden-Weinberger, U. and Beattie, G. (2022) Portrayals of autism in the British press: A corpus-based study. *Autism*, 27(4), 1092–1114. Available from: https://journals.sagepub.com/doi/full/10.1177/13623613221131752.

Lewin, N. and Akhtar, N. (2020) Neurodiversity and deficit perspectives in *The Washington Post*'s coverage of autism. *Disability and Society*, 36(5), 812–833.

McNulty, J. (2020, 14 May) Washington Post's depictions of autism shift from "cause and cure" to acceptance, study finds. UC Santa Cruz. Available from: https://news.ucsc.edu/2020/05/akhtar-post.html.

O'Dell, L. (2021, 29 August) What is the Spectrum 10K DNA study into autism – and why are autistic people concerned? *indy100*. Available from: www.indy100.com/news/spectrum-10k-study-autism-dna-b1910619.

Solutions Journalism Network (2023) What Is Solutions Journalism? Available from: www.solutionsjournalism.org/about/solutionsjournalism.

Spilsbury, M. (2023) *Diversity in Journalism: An Update on the Characteristics of Journalists*. Saffron Walden: National Council for the Training of Journalists. Available from: www.nctj.com/wp-content/uploads/2023/05/Diversity-in-journalism-2023-4WEB.pdf.

Conclusion

ADHD Aware (2023, May) BBC Panorama Episode – our response. Available from: https://adhdaware.org.uk/response-to-the-bbc-panorama-episode-private-adhd-clinics-exposed.

ADHD Foundation (2023, May) Response to BBC Panorama "Private ADHD Clinics Exposed". Available from: www.adhdfoundation.org.uk/2023/05/15/response-to-bbc-panorama-private-adhd-clinics-exposed.

American Psychiatric Association (2013) *Diagnostic and Statistical Manual of Mental Disorders: DSM-5*. Washington, DC: American Psychiatric Association.

Johnston, J. M., Foxx, R. M., Jacobson, J. W., Green, G. and Mulick, J. A. (2006) Positive behavior support and applied behavior analysis. *Behavior Analyst*, 29, 51–74.

Naish, J. (2023, February) Why are so many adults now being diagnosed with ADHD? *Mail Online*. Available from: www.dailymail.co.uk/health/article-11693601/Why-adults-diagnosed-ADHD-depth-look-condition.html.

Radomsky, A. R., Alcolado, G. M., Abramowitz, J. S., Alonso, P. et al. (2014) Part 1 – You can run but you can't hide: Intrusive thoughts on six continents. *Journal of Obsessive-Compulsive and Related Disorders*, 3(3), 269–279. Available from: https://doi.org/10.1016/j.jocrd.2013.09.002.

Rutherford, A. (2022) *Control: The Dark History and Troubling Present of Eugenics*. London: W&N.

Stephens, M. (2023, February) Fears teenagers self-diagnose autism and ADHD using TikTok. *The Telegraph*. Available from: www.telegraph.co.uk/news/2023/02/10/fears-teenagers-self-diagnose-autism-adhd-using-tiktok.